The Book of Jubilees

The Little Genesis, The Apocalypse of Moses

Joseph B. Lumpkin

The Book of Jubilees;

The Little Genesis, The Apocalypse of Moses

For information, authors should contact Fifth Estate, Post Office Box 116, Blountsville, AL 35031

First Edition

Printed on acid-free paper

Library of Congress Control Number:
2006900682
ISBN 1933580097

Fifth Estate, 2006

INTRODUCTION

The *Book of Jubilees,* also known as *The Little Genesis* and *The Apocalypse of Moses,* opens with an extraordinary claim of authorship. It is attributed to the very hand of Moses; penned while he was on Mount Sinai, as an angel of God dictated to him regarding those events that transpired from the beginning of the world. The story is written from the viewpoint of the angel. The angelic monolog takes place after the exodus of the children of Israel out of Egypt. The setting is atop Mount Sinai, where Moses was summoned by God. The text then unfolds as the angel reveals heaven's viewpoint of history. We are led through the creation of man, Adam's fall from grace, the union of fallen angels and earthly women, the birth of demonic offspring, the cleansing of the earth by flood, and the astonishing claim that man's very nature was somehow changed, bringing about a man with less sinful qualities than his antediluvian counterpart. The story goes on to fill in many details in Israel's history, ending at the point in time when the narrative itself takes place, after the exodus.

Scholars believe Jubilees was composed in the second century B.C. The Hebrew fragments found at Qumran are part of a Jewish library that contained other supporting literature such as the Book of Enoch and others. An analysis of the chronological development in the shapes of letters in the manuscripts confirms that Jubilees is pre-Christian in date and seems to have been penned between 100 and 200 B.C. Based on records of the High Priests at the time, we can further narrow the date of writing to between 140 and 100 B.C.

The book of Jubilees is also cited in the Qumran Damascus Document in pre-Christian texts.

The Book of Jubilees was originally written in Hebrew. The author was a Pharisee (a doctor of the law), or someone very familiar with scripture and religious law. Since the scrolls were found in what is assumed to be an Essene library, and were dated to the time the Essene community was active, the author was probably a member of that particular religious group. Jubilees represents a hyper-legalistic and midrashic tendency, which was part of the Essene culture at the time.

"Midrash" – refers to writings containing extra-legal material of anecdotal or allegorical nature, designed either to clarify historical material, or to teach a moral point.

Jubilees represents a midrash on Genesis 1:1 through Exodus 12:50 which depicts the episodes from creation with the observance of the Sabbath by the angels and men to Israel's escape from Egyptian bondage.

Although originally written in Hebrew, the Hebrew texts were completely lost until the find at Qumran. Fragments of Jubilees were discovered among the Dead Sea Scrolls. At least fourteen copies of the Book of Jubilees have been identified from caves 1, 2, 3 and 11 at Qumran. This makes it clear that the Book of Jubilees was a popular and probably authoritative text for the community whose library was concealed in the caves. These fragments are actually generations closer to the original copies than many books in our accepted Bible. Unfortunately, the fragments found at Qumran were only pieces of the texts and offered the briefest of glimpses of the entire book. The only complete versions of the Book of Jubilees are in Ethiopic, which in turn were translations of a Greek version.

Four Ethiopian manuscripts of Jubilees were found to be hundreds of years old. Of these, the fifteenth and sixteenth century texts are the truest and least corrupted when compared to the fragments found at Qumran. There are also citations of Jubilees in Syriac literature that may reflect a lost translation from Hebrew. Pieces of Latin translations have also been found.

Other fragments of a Greek version are quoted or referenced by Justin Martyr, Origen, Diodorus of Antioch, Isidore of Alexandria, Isidore of Seville, Eutychius, Patriarch of Alexandria, John of Malala, and Syncellus. This amount of various information and translations is enough to allow us to reconstruct the original to a great degree. The internal evidence of Jubilees shows very little tampering by Christians during its transmission and subsequent translations, thus allowing a clear view of certain Jewish beliefs being propagated at the time of its origin. By removing certain variances, we can isolate Christian alterations and mistakes in translations with a reasonable degree of confidence. Due to the poor condition of the fragments of Qumran, we may never be able to confirm certain key phrases in Hebrew. Thus, as with many texts, including those of our own Bible, in the end we must trust in the accuracy of the ancient translators.

It should be noted that the books of Jubilees, Enoch, and Jasher present stories of "The Watchers"; a group of angels sent to earth to record and teach, but who fell by their own lust and pride into a demonic state. Both Enoch and Jubilees refer to a solar-based calendar. This may show a conflict or transition at the time of their penning since Judaism now uses a lunar-based calendar.

Laws, rites, and functions are observed and noted in Jubilees. Circumcision is emphasized in both humans and angels. Angelic observance of Sabbath laws as well as parts of Jewish religious laws are said to have been observed in heaven before they were revealed to Moses.

To the Qumran community, complete obedience to the Laws of Moses entailed observing a series of holy days and festivals at a particular time according to a specific calendar. The calendar described in Jubilees is one of 364 days, divided into four seasons of three months each with thirteen weeks to a season. Each month had 30 days with one day added at certain times for each of the four seasons. With 52 weeks in a year, the festival and holy days recur at the same point each year. This calendar became a hallmark of an orthodox Qumran community.

The adherence to a specific calendar is one of many ways the Book of Jubilees shows the devotion to religious law. The law had been placed at the pinnacle of importance in the lives of the community at Qumran. All aspects of life were driven by a seemingly obsessive compliance to every jot and tittle of the law. The Book Of Jubilees confirms what can only be inferred from the books of Ezra, Nehemiah, and Zechariah, that the law and those who carried it out were supreme.

As the law took hold, by its nature, it crystallized the society. Free expression died, smothered under a mantle of hyperorthodoxy. Since free thought invited accusations of violations of the law or claims of heresy, prudence, a closed mind, and a silent voice prevailed. Free thought was limited to religious or apocryphal writings, which upheld the orthodox positions of the day. The silent period between Malachi and Mark may be a reflection of this stasis. Jubilees, Enoch, and other apocryphal books found in the Qumran caves are a triumph over the unimaginative mindset brought on by making religious law supreme and human expression contrary to law punishable by death. It may be an odd manifestation that such a burst of creativity was fueled by the very search for order that suppressed free thought in the first place.

The Book of Jubilees seems to be an attempt to answer and explain all questions left unanswered in the Book of Genesis as well as to bolster the position of the religious law. It attempts to trace the source of religious laws back to an ancient beginning thereby adding weight and sanction.

In the Book of Jubilees, we discover the origin of the wife of Cain. There is information offered about angels and the beginnings of the human race, how demons came into existence, and the place of Satan in the plans of God. Information is offered in an attempt to make perfect sense of the vagaries left in Genesis. For the defense of order and law and to maintain religious law as the center point of Jewish life, Jubilees was written as an answer to both pagan Greeks and liberal Jews. From the divine placement of law and order to its explanation of times and events, Jubilees is a panorama of legalism.

The name "Jubilees" comes from the division of time into eras known as Jubilees. One Jubilee occurs after the equivalent of forty-nine years, or seven Sabbaths or weeks of years has passed. It is the numerical perfection of seven sevens. In a balance and symmetry of years, the Jubilee occurs after seven cycles of seven or forty-nine years have been completed. Thus, the fiftieth year is a Jubilee year. Time is told by referencing the number of Jubilees that have transpired from the time the festival was first kept. For example, Israel entered Canaan at the close of the fiftieth jubilee, which is about 2450 BCE.

The obsession with time, dates, and the strict observance of festivals are all evidence of legalism taken to the highest level.

Based on the approximate time of writing, Jubilees was created in the time of the Maccabees, in the high priesthood of Hyrcanus. In this period of time the appearance of the Messiah and the rise of the Messianic kingdom were viewed as imminent. Followers were preparing themselves for the arrival of the Messiah and the establishment of His eternal kingdom.

Judaism was in contact with the Greek culture at the time. The Greeks were known to be philosophers and were developing processes of critical thinking. One objective of Jubilees was to defend Judaism against the attacks of the Hellenists and to prove that the law was logical, consistent, and valid. Attacks against paganism and non-believers are embedded in the text along with defense of the law and its consistency through proclamations of the law being observed by the angels in heaven from the beginning of creation.

Moral lessons are taught by use of the juxtaposition of the "satans" and their attempts to test and lead mankind into sin against the warning and advice of scriptural wisdom from Moses and his angels.

Mastema is mentioned only in The Book of Jubilees and in the Fragments of a Zadokite Work. Mastema is Satan. The name Mastema is derived from the Hebrew, "Mastim," meaning "adversary." The word occurs as singular and plural. The word is equivalent to Satan (adversary or accuser). This is similar to the chief Satan and his class of "satans" in 1 Enoch 40:7.

Mastema is subservient to God. His task is to tempt men to sin and if they do, he accuses them in the presence of the Throne of God. He and his minions lead men into sin but do not cause the sin. Once men have chosen to sin, they lead them from sin to destruction. Since man is given free will, sin is a choice, with Mastema simply encouraging and facilitating the decision. The choice, we can assume, is our own and the destruction that follows is "self-destruction."

Beliar is also mentioned. Beliar is the Greek name for Belial or Beliaal. The name in its Hebrew equivalent means "without value." This was a demon known by the Jews as the chief of all the devils. Belial is the leader of the Sons of Darkness. Belial is mentioned in the Fragments of a Zadokite fragment along with Mastema, which states that at the time of the Antichrist, Belial shall be let loose against Israel, as God spoke through Isaiah the prophet. Belial is sometimes presented as an agent of God's punishment although he is considered a "satan."

Although it is impossible to explore here in any detail the ramification of superhuman entities and their culpability in man's sin, it is important to mention that Judaism had no doctrine of original sin. The fall of Adam and Eve may have removed man from the perfect environment and the curses that followed may have shortened his lifespan, but propagation of sin through the bloodline was not considered. Sin seemed to affect only man and the animals he was given dominion over. Yet, man continued to sin, and to increase in his capacity and modes of sin. The explanation offered for man's inability to resist is the existence of fallen angels; spiritual, superhuman creations whose task it was to teach us but who now tempt and mislead men. In the end, the world declines and crumbles under the evil influence of the fallen angels turned demons called, "The Watchers."

With the establishment of the covenant between Abraham and God, we are told that God had appointed spirits to "mislead" all the nations but would not assign a spirit to lead or mislead the children of Isaac but God himself would be leading them.

Within the text are recurring numbers. Seven, being the number of perfection, is the most common. The number three is cited, being the number of completion. However, the number twenty-two occurs in the accounts of creation and lineage. It is worth noting that there are twenty-two letters in the Hebrew alphabet. The number twenty-two represents a type of Godly assignment or appointment. It is also the number of the perfect foundation and of the God-given language. It is presented within the text as a reminder that God established the ways of the Jews and gave the Hebrew language and writing first and only to the Jews.

The angels converse in Hebrew and it is the heavenly tongue. The law is written by God using this alphabet thus the law is also holy. All men spoke Hebrew until the time of Babel when it was lost. However, when Abraham dedicated himself to God, his ears were opened and his tongue was sanctified and Hebrew was again spoken and understood.

Finally, the entire text is based on the numbers of forty-nine and fifty. Forty-nine represents the pinnacle of perfection, being made up of seven times seven. The number fifty, which is the number of the Jubilee, is the number of grace. In this year slaves were to be set free, debts were forgiven, and grace filled the land and people.

Drawing from the theology and myths at the time, the book of Jubilees expands and embellishes on the creation story, the fall of Adam and Eve, and the fall of the angels. The expanded detail written into the text may have been one reason it was eventually rejected. However, the effects of the book can still be seen throughout the Judeo-Christian beliefs of today. The theology espoused in Jubilees can be seen in the angelology and demonology taught in the Christian churches of today and widely held by many Jews.

In an attempt to answer questions left unaddressed in Genesis the writer confronts the origin and identification of Cain's wife. According to The Book Of Jubilees, Cain married his sister, as did all of the sons of Adam and Eve, except Abel, who was murdered. This seemed offensive to some, since it flies in the face of the very law it was written to defend. Yet, this seemed to the writer to be the lesser of evils, given the problematic questions. Inbreeding is dismissed with the observation that the law was not fully given and understood then. The effects of the act were mute due to the purity of the newly created race.

The seeming discrepancy between divine command of Adam's death decree and the timing of his death is addressed. Seeing that Adam continued to live even after he ate the fruit, which was supposed to bring on his death, the writer set about to clarify God's actions. The problem is explained away in a single sentence. Since a day in heaven is as a thousand years on earth and Adam died having lived less than a thousand years this meant he died in the same heavenly day. Dying within the same day of the crime was acceptable.

In an astonishing parallel to the Book Of Enoch, written at about the same time as Jubilees, the Watchers, or sons of God mentioned in Genesis 6, fell from grace when they descended to earth and had sex with the daughters of men. In the Book of Enoch, the angels descended for the purpose of seducing the women of earth. However, in The Book Of Jubilee the angels were sent to teach men, but after living on earth for a while, were tempted by their own lust and fell. The offspring of this unholy union were bloodthirsty and cannibalistic giants. The Book of Jubilees indicates that the offspring were somehow different, yet they are divided into categories of the Naphidim (or Naphilim, depending or the transliteration), the Giants, and the Eljo. (Naphil are mentioned but this is the singular of Naphilim.)

As sin spread throughout the world and the minds of men were turned toward evil, God saw no alternative but to cleanse the earth with a flood and establish a "new nature" in man that does not have to sin. It is this new nature that the messiah will meet in mankind when He comes. As far as this author is aware, the re-creation of man's nature is mentioned in no other book. This idea of human nature being altered as it exited before the flood is found nowhere else but in Jubilees.

The angelic narrator tells us there were times in Israel's history when no evil existed and all men lived in accord. We are also told when and where the satans were allowed to attack and confound Israel. In this narrative, God uses his satans to harden the hearts of the Egyptians compelling them to pursue Israel and be destroyed.

The Book of Jubilees had other names throughout its history and propagation. "The Little Genesis" is another name given to this text. The description of "Little" does not refer to the size of the book, but to its canonical disposition.

"The Apocalypse of Moses" is another name denoting the same work. This title seems to have been used for only a short period of time. It refers to the revelation given to Moses as the recipient of all the knowledge disclosed in the book. The term "Apocalypse" means to make known or to reveal. With the exception of minor differences picked up through translation and copying, the three titles represent the same text.

About the Translation

The translation presented herein is based in part on that of R.H. Charles and his works of 1902 through 1913. Although the translation seems to be a faithful one, his scholarly tone, pedantry, and quasi-Elizabethan language made the text less than accessible. The pleonasm of the text as well as the ancient writer's tendency to repeat phrases for the sake of emphasis added to the general lack of readability. Furthermore, many of the verse breaks occurred in mid-sentence and certainly in mid-thought, adding confusion when viewing the text. All of these difficulties were corrected.

To aid in comprehension, it was decided that the text would be put through three phases of change. First, all verse breaks would be aligned with sentence breaks and with complete streams of thought when possible. Next, all archaic words and phrases would be replaced with their modern equivalent. Lastly, convoluted sentence structure would be clarified and rewritten. Notes of explanation and clarification are added in parentheses.

Due to the vast differences in societal structure and rules, certain phrases remained in their archaic form, seeing that they had no direct equivalence in our western culture. One such phrase is "uncovered the skirt." This phrase indicates the person was seen naked. In most cases it carries a connotation of intercourse. If one were to "uncover his father's skirt" it indicates the father's wife or concubine has been seen naked, usually with the intent of having sex with her.

When possible, the poetic flow of the text would be kept, but not at the expense of understanding. Various translations of each verse were referenced in order to compare and contrast differing viewpoints. The best rendering of the text was chosen and written into a more modern and readable format.

Since the book of Jubilees is written from the viewpoint of the angel narrating or dictating the text, when the words "I," "we," and "us" appear and the words are not readily connected to anyone within the sentence, it can be assumed the angel is referring to himself or the angelic host to which he belongs. When the narrator uses the word "you" he is referring to Moses, to whom the angel is speaking and dictating.

For simplicity's sake, it was decided to keep the word "soul" in the translation as related to the blood of animal and man. The phrase, "The soul is in the blood," will occur several times in the texts. It should be noted that the soul is the "life force," which came from God and belongs to God. It was considered sacred. It did not belong to man and was to be offered to God alone. Since blood represented life itself, it must be the centerpiece of any animal sacrifice. Sin or transgression of the law was punishable by death. Life must be offered as payment. The life force of an animal was offered in place of the life of the sinner. The blood of the animal represents this life.

Now, let us delve into this fascinating and illuminating book.

THE BOOK OF JUBILEES
THE LITTLE GENESIS, THE APOCALYPSE OF MOSES

This is the history of how the days were divided and of the days of the law and of the testimony, of the events of the years, and of the weeks of years, of their Jubilees throughout all the years of the world, as the Lord spoke to Moses on Mount Sinai when he went up to receive the tablets of the law and the commandment, according to the voice of God when he said to him, "Go up to the top of the Mount."

[Chapter *1*]

1 It happened in the first year of the exodus of the children of Israel out of Egypt, in the third month, on the sixteenth day of the month, that God spoke to Moses, saying, "Come up to Me on the Mountain, and I will give you two tablets of stone of the law and the commandment, which I have written, that you may teach them."

2 Moses went up into the mountain of God, and the glory of the Lord rested on Mount Sinai, and a cloud overshadowed it six days.

3 He called to Moses on the seventh day out of the middle of the cloud, and the appearance of the glory of the Lord was like a flame on the top of the mountain.

4 Moses was on the mountain forty days and forty nights, and God taught him the earlier and the later history of the division of all the days of the law and of the testimony.

5 He said, "Open your heart to every word which I shall speak to you on this mountain, and write them in a book in order that their generations may see how I have not forsaken them for all the evil which they have committed when they transgressed the covenant which I establish between Me and you for their generations this day on Mount Sinai.

6 It will come to pass when all these things come on them, that they will recognize that I am more righteous than they in all their judgments and in all their actions, and they will recognize that I have truly been with them.

7 Write all these words for yourself which I speak to you today, for I know their rebellion and their stubbornness, before I brought them into the land of which I swore to their fathers, to Abraham and to Isaac and to Jacob, saying, " Unto your offspring will I give a land flowing with milk and honey.

8 They will eat and be satisfied, and they will turn to strange gods, to gods that cannot deliver them from any of their tribulation, and this witness shall be heard for a witness against them.

9 They will forget all My commandments, even all that I command them, and they will walk in the ways of the Gentiles, and after their uncleanness, and after their shame, and will serve their gods, and these will prove to them an offence and a tribulation and an sickness and a trap.

10 Many will perish and they will be taken captive, and will fall into the hands of the enemy, because they have forsaken My laws and My commandments, and the festivals of My covenant, and My sabbaths, and My holy place which I have made holy for Myself in their presence, and My tabernacle, and My sanctuary, which I have made holy for Myself in the midst of the land, that I should set My name on it, that it should reside there.

11 They will make themselves high places and places of worship and graven images. Each will worship graven images of his own making, Thus they will go astray. They will sacrifice their children to demons, and to all errors their hearts can work.

12 I will send witnesses to them that I may testify against them, but they will not hear. They will kill the witnesses. They will persecute those who seek the law, and they will abolish and change everything (in the Law) so as to work evil before My eyes.

13 I will hide My face from them. I will deliver them into the hand of the Gentiles. They will be captured like prey for their eating. I will remove them from the out of the land. I will scatter them among the Gentiles.

14 And they will forget My law and all My commandments and all My judgments. They will go astray regarding the observance of new moons, and sabbaths, and festivals, and jubilees, and laws.

15 After this they will turn to Me from among the Gentiles with all their heart and with all their soul and with all their strength, and I will gather them from among all the Gentiles, and they will seek me. I shall be found by them when they seek me with all their heart and with all their soul.

16 I will allow them to see abounding peace with righteousness. I will remove them, the plant of uprightness, with all My heart and with all My soul, and they shall be for a blessing and not for a curse, and they shall be the head and not the tail.

17 I will build My sanctuary among them, and I will dwell with them, and I will be their God and they shall be My people in truth and righteousness.

18 I will not forsake them nor fail them; for I am the Lord their God."

19 Moses fell on his face and prayed and said, 'O Lord my God, do not forsake Your people and Your inheritance, so that they should wander in the error of their hearts, and do not deliver them into the hands of their enemies, the Gentiles, so that they should rule over them and cause them to sin against You.

20 Let your mercy, O Lord, be lifted up on Your people, and create in them an upright spirit, and let not the spirit of Beliar rule over them to accuse them before You, and to ensnare them from all the paths of righteousness, so that they may perish from before Your face.

21 But they are Your people and Your inheritance, which You have delivered with Your great power from the hands of the Egyptians, create in them a clean heart and a holy spirit, and let them not be ensnared in their sins from now on until eternity."

22 The Lord said to Moses, "I know their contrariness and their thoughts and their stubbornness, and they will not be obedient until they confess their own sin and the sin of their fathers.

23 After this they will turn to Me in all uprightness and with all their heart and with all their soul, and I will circumcise the foreskin of their heart and the foreskin of the heart of their offspring, and I will create in them a holy spirit, and I will cleanse them so that they shall not turn away from Me from that day to eternity.

24 And their souls will cling to Me and to all My commandments, and they will fulfill My commandments, and I will be their Father and they shall be My children.

25 They all shall be called children of the living God, and every angel and every spirit shall know, yes, they shall know that these are My children, and that I am their Father in uprightness and righteousness, and that I love them.

26 Write down for yourself all these words which I say to you on this mountain, from the first to the last, which shall come to pass in all the divisions of the days in the law and in the testimony and in the weeks and the jubilees to eternity, until I descend and dwell with them throughout eternity."

27 He said to the angel of the presence (of the Lord), "Write for Moses from the beginning of creation until My sanctuary has been built among them for all eternity.

28 The Lord will appear to the eyes of all, and all shall know that I am the God of Israel and the Father of all the children of Jacob, and King on Mount Zion for all eternity. And Zion and Jerusalem shall be holy."

29 The angel of the presence (of the Lord) who went before the camp of Israel took the tables of the divisions of the years, written from the time of the creation, concerning the law and the testimony of the weeks of the jubilees, according to the individual years, according to the numbering of all the jubilees, from the day of the new creation when the heavens and the earth shall be renewed and all their creation according to the powers of the heaven, and according to all the creation of the earth, until the sanctuary of the Lord shall be made in Jerusalem on Mount Zion, and all the stars and planets be renewed for healing, peace, and blessing for all the elect of Israel, and that this is the way it may be from that day and to all the days of the earth.

[Chapter *2*]

1 The angel of the presence (of the Lord) spoke to Moses according to the word of the Lord, saying, "Write the complete history of the creation, how in six days the Lord God finished all His works and all that He created, and kept Sabbath on the seventh day and made it holy for all ages, and appointed it as a sign for all His works.

2 For on the first day He created the heavens which are above and the earth and the waters and all the spirits which serve before him which are the angels of the presence (of the Lord), and the angels of sanctification, and the angels of the spirit of fire, and the angels of the spirit of the winds, and the angels of the spirit of the clouds, and of darkness, and of snow and of hail and of white frost, and the angels of the voices and of the thunder and of the lightning, and the angels of the spirits of cold and of heat, and of winter and of spring and of autumn and of summer and of all the spirits of his creatures which are in the heavens and on the earth, He created the bottomless pit and the darkness, evening and night, and the light, dawn and day, which He has prepared in the knowledge of His heart.

3 When we saw His works, we praised Him, and worshiped before Him because of all His works; for seven great works did He create on the first day.

4 On the second day He created the sky between the waters (above and below), and the waters were divided on that day. Half of them went up above the sky and half of them went down below the sky that was in the middle over the face of the whole earth. And this was the only work God created on the second day.

5 On the third day He commanded the waters to pass from off the face of the whole earth into one place, and the dry land to appear.

6 The waters did as He commanded them, and they receded from off the face of the earth into one place, and the dry land appeared.

7 On that day He created for them all the seas according to their separate gathering-places, and all the rivers, and the gatherings of the waters in the mountains and on all the earth, and all the lakes, and all the dew of the earth, and the seed which is sown, and all sprouting things, and fruit-bearing trees, and trees of the wood, and the garden of Eden, in Eden and throughout. These four great works God created on the third day.

8 On the fourth day He created the sun and the moon and the stars, and set them in the sky of the heaven, to give light on all the earth, and to rule over the day and the night, and divide the light from the darkness.

9 God appointed the sun to be a great sign on the earth for days and for sabbaths and for months and for feasts and for years and for sabbaths of years and for jubilees and for all seasons of the years.

10 And it divides the light from the darkness for prosperity that all things may prosper which sprout and grow on the earth. These three kinds He made on the fourth day.

11 On the fifth day He created great sea monsters in the depths of the waters, for these were the first things of flesh that were created by his hands, the fish and everything that moves in the waters, and everything that flies, the birds and all their kind.

12 And the sun rose above them to make them prosper, and the sun rose above everything that was on the earth, everything that sprouts out of the earth, and all fruit-bearing trees, and all flesh.

13 He created these three kinds on the fifth day. On the sixth day He created all the animals of the earth, and all cattle, and everything that moves on the earth.

14 After all this He created mankind. He created a man and a woman, and gave him dominion over all that is on the earth, and in the seas, and over everything that flies, and over beasts, and over cattle, and over everything that moves on the earth, and over the whole earth, and over all this He gave him dominion.

15 He created these four kinds on the sixth day. And there were altogether two and twenty kinds.

16 He finished all his work on the sixth day. That is all that is in the heavens and on the earth, and in the seas and in the abysses, and in the light and in the darkness, and in everything.

17 He gave us a great sign, the Sabbath day, that we should work six days, but keep Sabbath on the seventh day from all work.

18 All the angels of the presence (of the Lord), and all the angels of sanctification, these two great types of angels He has told to tell us to keep the Sabbath with Him in heaven and on earth.

19 And He said to us, "Look, I will separate to Myself a people from among all the peoples, and these shall keep the Sabbath day, and I will sanctify them to Myself as My people, and will bless them; as I have sanctified the Sabbath day and do sanctify it to Myself, even so will I bless them, and they shall be My people and I will be their God.

20 I have chosen the offspring of Jacob from among all that I have seen, and have written him down as My first-born son, and have sanctified him to Myself forever and ever; and I will teach them the Sabbath day, that they may keep Sabbath on it from all work."

21 He created in it a sign in accordance with which they should keep Sabbath with us on the seventh day, to eat and to drink, and to bless Him who has created all things as He has blessed and sanctified to Himself a particular, exclusive people above all peoples, and that they should keep Sabbath together with us.

22 He caused His commands to rise up as a sweet odor acceptable before Him all the days.

23 There were two and twenty heads (representatives) of mankind from Adam to Jacob, and two and twenty kinds of work (creation) were made until the seventh day; this is blessed and holy; and the former also is blessed and holy; and this one serves with that one for sanctification and blessing.

24 Jacob and his offspring were granted that they should always be the blessed and holy ones of the first testimony and law, even as He had sanctified and blessed the Sabbath day on the seventh day.

25 He created heaven and earth and everything that He created in six days, and God made the seventh day holy, for all His works; therefore He commanded on its behalf that, whoever does any work on it shall die, and that he who defiles it shall surely die.

26 Because of this, command the children of Israel to observe this day that they may keep it holy and not do on it any work, and not to defile it, as it is holier than all other days.

27 And whoever profanes it shall surely die, and whoever does any work on it shall surely die eternally, that the children of Israel may observe this day throughout their generations, and not be rooted out of the land; for it is a holy day and a blessed day.

28 Every one who observes it and keeps Sabbath on it from all his work will be holy and blessed throughout all days as we are blessed.

29 Declare and say to the children of Israel the law of this day that they should keep Sabbath on it, and that they should not forsake it in the error of their hearts; and that it is not lawful to do any work on it which is not suitable, to do their own pleasure on it, and that they should not prepare anything to be eaten or drunk on it, and that it is not lawful to draw water, or bring in or take out through their gates any burden which they had not prepared for themselves on the sixth day in their dwellings.

30 They shall not bring or take anything from house to house on that day; for that day is more holy and blessed than any jubilee day of the jubilees; on this we kept Sabbath in the heavens before it was made known to any flesh to keep Sabbath on the earth.

31 The Creator of all things blessed it, but He did not sanctify all peoples and nations to keep Sabbath, but Israel alone, them alone He permitted to eat and drink and to keep Sabbath on the earth.

32 And the Creator of all things blessed this day which He had created for blessing and holiness and glory above all days.

33 This law and testimony was given to the children of Israel as a law forever to their generations.

[Chapter 3]

1 On the sixth day of the second week, according to the word of God, we brought to Adam all the beasts, and all the cattle, and all the birds, and everything that moves on the earth, and everything that moves in the water, according to their kinds, and according to their types, the beasts on the first day; the cattle on the second day; the birds on the third day; and all that moves on the earth on the fourth day; and that moves in the water on the fifth day.

2 And Adam named them all by their respective names. As he called them, so was their name.

3 On these five days Adam saw all these, male and female, according to every kind that was on the earth, but he was alone and found no helpmate.

4 The Lord said to us, "It is not good that the man should be alone, let us make a helpmate for him."

5 And the Lord our God caused a deep sleep to fall on him, and he slept, and He took from Adam a rib from among his ribs for the woman, and this rib was the origin of the woman. And He built up the flesh in its place, and built the woman.

6 He awakened Adam out of his sleep and on awakening he rose on the sixth day, and He brought her to him, and he knew her, and said to her, "This is now bone of my bones and flesh of my flesh; she shall be called my wife; because she was taken from her husband."

7 Therefore shall man and wife become one and therefore shall a man leave his father and his mother, and cling to his wife, and they shall be one flesh.

8 In the first week Adam was created, and from his rib, his wife. In the second week God showed her to him, and for this reason the commandment was given to keep in their defilement. A male should be purified in seven days, and for a female twice seven days.

9 After Adam had completed forty days in the land where he had been created, we brought him into the garden of Eden to till and keep it, but his wife we brought in on the eightieth day, and after this she entered into the garden of Eden.

10 And for this reason the commandment is written on the heavenly tablets in regard to her that gives birth, "If she bears a male, she shall remain unclean for seven days according to the first week of days, and thirty-three days shall she remain in the blood of her purifying, and she shall not touch any holy thing, nor enter into the sanctuary, until she completes these days which are decreed in the case of a male child.

11 But in the case of a female child she shall remain unclean two weeks of days, according to the first two weeks, and sixty-six days in the blood of her purification, and they will be in all eighty days."

12 When she had completed these eighty days we brought her into the Garden of Eden, for it is holier than all the earth besides and every tree that is planted in it is holy.

13 Therefore, there was ordained regarding her who bears a male or a female child the statute of those days that she should touch no holy thing, nor enter into the sanctuary until these days for the male or female child are completed.

14 This is the law and testimony that was written down for Israel, in order that they should observe it all the days.

15 In the first week of the first jubilee, Adam and his wife were in the garden of Eden for seven years tilling and keeping it, and we gave him work and we instructed him to do everything that is suitable for tillage.

16 And he tilled the garden, and was naked and did not realize it, and was not ashamed. He protected the garden from the birds and beasts and cattle. He gathered its fruit, and ate, and put aside that which was left over for himself and for his wife.

17 After the completion of exactly seven years there, and in the second month, on the seventeenth day of the month, the serpent came and approached the woman, and the serpent said to the woman, "Has God commanded you saying, you shall not eat of every tree of the garden?"

18 She said to it, God said to us, of all the fruit of the trees of the garden, eat; but of the fruit of the tree which is in the middle of the garden God said to us, you shall not eat of it, neither shall you touch it, or you shall die."

19 The serpent said to the woman, "You shall not surely die. God does know that on the day you shall eat of it, your eyes will be opened, and you will be as gods, and you will know good and evil.

20 And the woman saw the tree that it was beautiful and pleasant to the eye, and that its fruit was good for food, and she took of it and ate.

21 First, she covered her shame with fig leaves and then she gave the fruit to Adam and he ate, and his eyes were opened, and he saw that he was naked.

22 He took fig leaves and sewed them together, and made an apron for himself, and covered his shame.

23 God cursed the serpent, and was very angry at it forever.

24 And He was very angry with the woman, because she listened to the voice of the serpent, and ate; and He said to her, "I will vastly multiply your sorrow and your pains, in sorrow you will bring forth children, and your master shall be your husband, and he will rule over you."

25 To Adam also he said, " Because you have listened to the voice of your wife, and have eaten of the tree of which I commanded you not to eat, cursed be the ground for your sake, thorns and thistles shall it produce for you, and you will eat your bread in the sweat of your face, until you return to the earth from where you were taken; for earth you are, and to earth will you return."

26 And He made for them coats of skin, and clothed them, and sent them out from the Garden of Eden.

27 On that day on which Adam went out from the Garden, he offered as a sweet odor an offering, frankincense, incense, and sweet spice, and spices in the morning with the rising of the sun from the day when he covered his shame.

28 On that day was closed the mouth of all beasts, and of cattle, and of birds, and of whatever walks, and of whatever moves, so that they could no longer speak, for they had all spoken one with another with one dialect and with one language.

29 All flesh that was in the Garden of Eden He sent out of the Garden of Eden, and all flesh was scattered according to its kinds, and according to its types to the places that had been created for them.

30 Of all the beasts and cattle only to Adam alone He gave the ability to cover his shame.

31 Because of this, it is prescribed on the heavenly tablets as touching all those who know the judgment of the law, that they should cover their shame, and should not uncover themselves as the Gentiles uncover themselves.

32 On the new moon of the fourth month, Adam and his wife went out from the Garden of Eden, and they dwelt in the land of Elda in the land of their creation.

33 And Adam called the name of his wife Eve.

34 And they had no son until the first jubilee, and after this he knew her.

35 Now he tilled the land as he had been instructed in the Garden of Eden.

[Chapter 4]

1 In the third week in the second jubilee she gave birth to Cain, and in the fourth (week of the) jubilee she gave birth to Abel, and in the fifth (week of the) jubilee she gave birth to her daughter Awan. (A week is seven years.)

2 In the first year of the third jubilee, Cain killed Abel because God accepted the sacrifice of Abel, and did not accept the offering of Cain.

3 And he killed him in the field, and his blood cried from the ground to heaven, complaining because he had killed him.

4 The Lord blamed Cain, because he had killed Abel, and He made him a fugitive on the earth because of the blood of his brother, and He cursed him on the earth.

5 Because of this it is written on the heavenly tablets, "Cursed is he who kills his neighbor treacherously, and let all who have seen and heard say, 'So be it', and the man who has seen and not reported it, let him be accursed as the one committing it."

6 For this reason we announce when we come before the Lord our God all the sin that is committed in heaven and on earth, and in light and in darkness, and everywhere.

7 And Adam and his wife mourned for Abel four weeks of years, and in the fourth year of the fifth week they became joyful, and Adam knew his wife again, and she gave birth to a son, and he called his name Seth, for he said "God has raised up a second offspring to us on the earth instead of Abel; for Cain killed him."

8 In the sixth week he begat his daughter Azura.

9 And Cain took Awan his sister to be his wife and she gave birth to Enoch at the close of the fourth jubilee.

10 In the first year of the first week of the fifth jubilee, houses were built on the earth, and Cain built a city, and called its name after the name of his son Enoch.

11 Adam knew Eve his wife and she gave birth to a total of nine sons. In the fifth week of the fifth jubilee Seth took Azura his sister to be his wife, and in the fourth year of the sixth week she gave birth to Enos.

12 He began to call on the name of the Lord on the earth.

13 In the seventh jubilee in the third week Enos took Noam his sister to be his wife, and she gave birth to a son in the third year of the fifth week, and he called his name Kenan.

14 At the close of the eighth jubilee Kenan took Mualeleth his sister to be his wife, and she gave birth to a son in the ninth jubilee, in the first week in the third year of this week, and he called his name Mahalalel.

15 In the second week of the tenth jubilee Mahalalel took to him to wife Dinah, the daughter of Barakiel the daughter of his father's brother, and she gave birth to a son in the third week in the sixth year, and he called his name Jared, for in his days the angels of the Lord descended on the earth, those who are named the Watchers, that they should instruct the children of men, and that they should do judgment and uprightness on the earth.

16 In the eleventh jubilee Jared took to himself a wife, and her name was Baraka, the daughter of Rasujal, a daughter of his father's brother, in the fourth week of this jubilee, and she gave birth to a son in the fifth week, in the fourth year of the jubilee, and he called his name Enoch.

17 He was the first among men that are born on earth who learned writing and knowledge and wisdom and who wrote down the signs of heaven according to the order of their months in a book, that men might know the seasons of the years according to the order of their separate months.

18 He was the first to write a testimony and he testified to the sons of men among the generations of the earth, and recounted the weeks of the jubilees, and made known to them the days of the years, and set in order the months and recounted the Sabbaths of the years as we made them, known to him.

19 And what was and what will be he saw in a vision of his sleep, as it will happen to the children of men throughout their generations until the day of judgment; he saw and understood everything, and wrote his testimony, and placed the testimony on earth for all the children of men and for their generations.

20 In the twelfth jubilee, in the seventh week of it, he took to himself a wife, and her name was Edna, the daughter of Danel, the daughter of his father's brother, and in the sixth year in this week she gave birth to a son and he called his name Methuselah.

21 He was with the angels of God these six jubilees of years, and they showed him everything that is on earth and in the heavens, the rule of the sun, and he wrote down everything.

22 And he testified to the Watchers, who had sinned with the daughters of men; for these had begun to unite themselves, so as to be defiled with the daughters of men, and Enoch testified against them all.

23 And he was taken from among the children of men, and we conducted him into the Garden of Eden in majesty and honor, and there he wrote down the condemnation and judgment of the world, and all the wickedness of the children of men.

24 Because of it God brought the waters of the flood on all the land of Eden; for there he was set as a sign and that he should testify against all the children of men, that he should recount all the deeds of the generations until the day of condemnation.

25 He burnt the incense of the sanctuary, even sweet spices acceptable before the Lord on the Mount.

26 For the Lord has four places on the earth, the Garden of Eden, and the Mount of the East, and this mountain on which you are this day, Mount Sinai, and Mount Zion which will be sanctified in the new creation for a sanctification of the earth; through it will the earth be sanctified from all its guilt and its uncleanness throughout the generations of the world.

27 In the fourteenth jubilee Methuselah took to himself a wife, Edna the daughter of Azrial, the daughter of his father's brother, in the third week, in the first year of this week, and he begat a son and called his name Lamech.

28 In the fifteenth jubilee in the third week Lamech took to himself a wife, and her name was Betenos the daughter of Baraki'il, the daughter of his father's brother, and in this week she gave birth to a son and he called his name Noah, saying, "This one will comfort me for my trouble and all my work, and for the ground which the Lord has cursed."

29 At the close of the nineteenth jubilee, in the seventh week in the sixth year of it, Adam died, and all his sons buried him in the land of his creation, and he was the first to be buried in the earth.

30 He lacked seventy years of one thousand years, because one thousand years are as one day in the testimony of the heavens. Therefore was it written concerning the tree of knowledge, "On the day that you eat of it you shall die." Because of this he did not complete the one thousand years but instead he died during it.

31 At the close of this jubilee Cain was killed after him in the same year; because his house fell on him and he died in the middle of his house, and he was killed by its stones. With a stone he had killed Abel, and by a stone he was killed in righteous judgment.

32 For this reason it was ordained on the heavenly tablets, with the instrument with which a man kills his neighbor with the same shall he be killed. In the same manner that he wounded him, in like manner shall they deal with him."

33 In the twenty-fifth jubilee Noah took to himself a wife, and her name was Emzara, the daughter of Rake'el, the daughter of his father's brother, in the first year in the fifth week, and in the third year of it she gave birth to Shem, in the fifth year of it she gave birth to Ham, and in the first year in the sixth week she gave birth to Japheth.

[Chapter 5]

1 When the children of men began to multiply on the face of the earth and daughters were born to them, and the angels of God saw them on a certain year of this jubilee, that they were beautiful, and they took themselves wives of all whom they chose, and they gave birth to their sons and they were giants.

2 Because of them lawlessness increased on the earth and all flesh corrupted its way. Men and cattle and beasts and birds and everything that walked on the earth were all corrupted in their ways and their orders, and they began to devour each other. Lawlessness increased on the earth and the imagination and thoughts of all men were continually, totally evil.

3 God looked on the earth, and saw it was corrupt, and all flesh had corrupted its orders, and all that were on the earth had committed all manner of evil before His eyes.

4 He said that He would destroy man and all flesh on the face of the earth that He had created.

5 But Noah found grace before the eyes of the Lord.

6 And against the angels whom He had sent on the earth, He had boiling anger, and He gave commandment to root them out of all their dominion, and He commanded us to bind them in the depths of the earth, and look, they are bound in the middle of the earth, and are kept separate.

7 And against their sons went out a command from His mouth that they should be killed with the sword, and be left under heaven.

8 He said, "My spirit shall not always abide on man; for they also are flesh and their days shall be one hundred and twenty years."

9 He sent His sword into their presence that each should kill his neighbor, and they began to kill each other until they all fell by the sword and were destroyed from the earth.

10 And their fathers were witnesses of their destruction, and after this they were bound in the depths of the earth forever, until the day of the great condemnation, when judgment is executed on all those who have corrupted their ways and their works before the Lord.

11 He destroyed all wherever they were, and there was not one left of them whom He judged according to all their wickedness.

12 Through His work He made a new and righteous nature, so that they should not sin in their whole nature forever, but should be all righteous each in his own way always.

13 The judgment of all is ordained and written on the heavenly tablets in righteousness, even the judgment of all who depart from the path that is ordained for them to walk; and if they do not walk it, judgment is written down for every creature and for every kind.

14 There is nothing in heaven or on earth, or in light or in darkness, or in the abode of the dead or in the depth, or in the place of darkness that is not judged. All their judgments are ordained and written and engraved.

15 He will judge all, the great according to his greatness, and the small according to his smallness, and each according to his way.

16 He is not one who will regard the position of any person, nor is He one who will receive gifts, if He says that He will execute judgment on each.

17 If one gave everything that is on the earth, He will not regard the gifts or the person of any, nor accept anything at his hands, for He is a righteous judge.

18 Of the children of Israel it has been written and ordained, if they turn to him in righteousness He will forgive all their transgressions and pardon all their sins. It is written and ordained that He will show mercy to all who turn from all their guilt once each year.

19 And as for all those who corrupted their ways and their thoughts before the flood, no person was acceptable to God except Noah. His sons were saved in deference to him, and these God kept from the waters of the flood on his account; for Noah's heart was righteous in all his ways. He upheld the laws and did as God commanded him and he had not departed from anything that was ordained for him.

20 The Lord said that he would destroy everything on the earth, both men and cattle, and beasts, and birds of the air, and that which moves on the earth.

21 And He commanded Noah to make an ark, so that he might save himself from the waters of the flood.

22 And Noah made the ark in all respects as He commanded him, in the twenty-seventh jubilee of years, in the fifth week in the fifth year on the new moon of the first month.

23 He entered in the sixth year of it, in the second month, on the new moon of the second month, until the sixteenth; and he entered, and all that we brought to him, into the ark, and the Lord closed it from the outside on the seventeenth evening.

24 And the Lord opened seven floodgates of heaven, and He opened the mouths of the fountains of the great deep, seven mouths in number.

25 And the floodgates began to pour down water from the heaven forty days and forty closets, And the fountains of the deep also sent up waters, until the whole world was full of water.

26 The waters increased on the earth, by fifteen cubits (a cubit is about **18** inches) the waters rose above all the high mountains. And the ark was lift up from the earth. And it moved on the face of the waters.

27 And the water covered the face of the earth five months, which is one hundred and fifty days.

28 And the ark went and rested on the top of Lubar, one of the mountains of Ararat.

29 On the new moon in the fourth month the fountains of the great deep were closed and the floodgates of heaven were restrained; and on the new moon of the seventh month all the mouths of the bottomless gulfs of the earth were opened, and the water began to flow down into the deep below.

30 On the new moon of the tenth month the tops of the mountains were seen, and on the new moon of the first month the earth became visible.

31 The waters disappeared from the earth in the fifth week in the seventh year of it, and on the seventeenth day in the second month the earth was dry.

32 On the twenty-seventh of it he opened the ark, and sent out beasts, and cattle, and birds, and every moving thing.

[Chapter *6*]

1 On the new moon of the third month he went out of the ark, and built an altar on that mountain.

2 And he made atonement for the earth, and took a kid and made atonement by its blood for all the guilt of the earth; for every thing that had been on it had been destroyed, except those that were in the ark with Noah.

3 He placed the fat of it on the altar, and he took an ox, and a goat, and a sheep and kids, and salt, and a turtle-dove, and the young of a dove, and placed a burnt sacrifice on the altar, and poured on it an offering mingled with oil, and sprinkled wine and sprinkled frankincense over everything, and caused a good and pleasing odor to arise, acceptable before the Lord.

4 And the Lord smelled the good and pleasing odor, and He made a covenant with Noah that there should not be any more floods to destroy the earth; that all the days of the earth seed-time and harvest should never cease; cold and heat, and summer and winter, and day and night should not change their order, nor cease forever.

5 "Increase and multiply on the earth, and become many, and be a blessing on it. I will inspire the fear of you and the dread of you in everything that is on earth and in the sea.

6 Look, I have given you all beasts, and all winged things, and everything that moves on the earth, and the fish in the waters, and all things for food; as the green herbs, I have given you all things to eat.

7 But you shall not eat anything live or with blood in it, for the life of all flesh is in the blood, or your blood of your lives will be required. At the hand of every man, at the hand of every beast will I require the blood of man.

8 Whoever sheds man's blood by man shall his blood be shed, for in the image of God He made man.

9 Increase, and multiply on the earth."

10 Noah and his sons swore that they would not eat any blood that was in any flesh, and he made a covenant before the Lord God forever throughout all the generations of the earth in this month.

11 Because of this He spoke to you that you should make a covenant with the children of Israel with an oath. In this month, on the mountain you should sprinkle blood on them because of all the words of the covenant, which the Lord made with them forever.

12 This testimony is written concerning you that you should observe it continually, so that you should not eat on any day any blood of beasts or birds or cattle during all the days of the earth, and the man who eats the blood of beast or of cattle or of birds during all the days of the earth, he and his offspring shall be rooted out of the land.

13 And you will command the children of Israel to eat no blood, so that their names and their offspring may be before the Lord our God continually.

14 There is no limit of days, for this law. It is forever. They shall observe it throughout their generations, so that they may continue supplicating on your behalf with blood before the altar; every day and at the time of morning and evening they shall seek forgiveness on your behalf perpetually before the Lord that they may keep it and not be rooted out.

15 And He gave to Noah and his sons a sign that there should not again be a flood on the earth.

16 He set His bow (a rainbow) in the cloud as a sign of the eternal covenant that there should never again be a flood on the earth to destroy it for all the days of the earth.

17 For this reason it is ordained and written on the heavenly tablets, that they should celebrate the feast of weeks in this month once a year, to renew the covenant every year.

18 This whole festival was celebrated in heaven from the day of creation until the days of Noah, which were twenty-six jubilees and five weeks of years. Noah and his sons observed it for seven jubilees and one week of years, until the day of Noah's death. From the day of Noah's death his sons did away with it until the days of Abraham, and they ate blood.

19 But Abraham observed it, and Isaac and Jacob and his children observed it up to your days, and in your days the children of Israel forgot it until you celebrated it anew on this mountain.

20 Command the children of Israel to observe this festival in all their generations for a commandment to them, one day in the year in this month they shall celebrate the festival.

21 For it is the feast of weeks and the feast of first-fruits, this feast is twofold and of a double nature, according to what is written and engraved concerning it, celebrate it.

22 For I have written in the book of the first law, in that which I have written for you, that you should celebrate it in its season, one day in the year, and I explained to you its sacrifices that the children of Israel should remember and should celebrate it throughout their generations in this month, the same day in every year.

23 On the new moon of the first month, and on the new moon of the fourth month, and on the new moon of the seventh month, and on the new moon of the tenth month are the days of remembrance, and the days of the seasons in the four divisions of the year. These are written and ordained as a testimony forever.

24 Noah ordained them for himself as feasts for the generations forever, so that they have become a memorial to him.

25 On the new moon of the first month he was told to make for himself an ark, and on that day the earth was dry and he saw from the opened ark, the earth. On the new moon of the fourth month the mouths of the depths of the bottomless pit beneath were closed.

26 On the new moon of the seventh month all the mouths of the abysses of the earth were opened, and the waters began to descend into them.

27 On the new moon of the tenth month the tops of the mountains were seen, and Noah was glad.

28 Because of this he ordained them for himself as feasts for a memorial forever, and thus are they ordained.

29 And they placed them on the heavenly tablets, each had thirteen weeks; from one to another passed their memorial, from the first to the second, and from the second to the third, and from the third to the fourth.

30 All the days of the commandment will be two and fifty weeks of days, and these will make the entire year complete. Thus it is engraved and ordained on the heavenly tablets.

31 And there is no neglecting this commandment for a single year or from year to year.

32 Command the children of Israel that they observe the years according to this counting, three hundred and sixty-four days, and these will constitute a complete year, and they will not disturb its time from its days and from its feasts; for every thing will fall out in them according to their testimony, and they will not leave out any day nor disturb any feasts.

33 But if they neglect and do not observe them according to His commandment, then they will disturb all their seasons and the years will be dislodged from this order, and they will neglect their established rules.

34 And all the children of Israel will forget and will not find the path of the years, and will forget the new moons, and seasons, and sabbaths and they will wrongly determine all the order of the years.

35 For I know and from now on will I declare it to you, and it is not of my own devising; for the book lies written in the presence of me, and on the heavenly tablets the division of days is ordained, or they forget the feasts of the covenant and walk according to the feasts of the Gentiles after their error and after their ignorance.

36 For there will be those who will assuredly make observations of the moon and how it disturbs the seasons and comes in from year to year ten days too soon.

37 For this reason the years will come upon them when they disturb (misinterpret) the order, and make an abominable day the day of testimony, and an unclean day a feast day, and they will confound all the days, the holy with the unclean, and the unclean day with the holy; for they will go wrong as to the months and sabbaths and feasts and jubilees.

38 For this reason I command and testify to you that you may testify to them; for after your death your children will disturb them, so that they will not make the year three hundred and sixty-four days only, and for this reason they will go wrong as to the new moons and seasons and sabbaths and festivals, and they will eat all kinds of blood with all kinds of flesh.

[Chapter 7]

1 In the seventh week in the first year of it, in this jubilee, Noah planted vines on the mountain on which the ark had rested, named Lubar, one of the Ararat Mountains, and they produced fruit in the fourth year, and he guarded their fruit, and gathered it in that year in the seventh month.

2 He made wine from it and put it into a vessel, and kept it until the fifth year, until the first day, on the new moon of the first month.

3 And he celebrated with joy the day of this feast, and he made a burnt sacrifice to the Lord, one young ox and one ram, and seven sheep, each a year old, and a kid of the goats, that he might make atonement thereby for himself and his sons.

4 He prepared the kid first, and placed some of its blood on the flesh that was on the altar that he had made, and all the fat he laid on the altar where he made the burnt sacrifice, and the ox and the ram and the sheep, and he laid all their flesh on the altar.

5 He placed all their offerings mingled with oil on it, and afterwards he sprinkled wine on the fire which had previously been made on the altar, and he placed incense on the altar and caused a sweet odor to rise up which was acceptable before the Lord his God.

6 And he rejoiced and he and his children drank the wine with joy.

7 It was evening, and he went into his tent, and being drunken he lay down and slept, and was uncovered in his tent as he slept.

8 And Ham saw Noah his father naked, and went out and told his two brothers (ridiculed his father to his two brothers) who were outside.

9 Shem took his garment and arose, he and Japheth, and they placed the garment on their shoulders and went backward and covered the shame of their father, and their faces were backward.

10 Noah awoke from sleep and knew all (abuse) that his younger son had done to him. He cursed him saying, "Cursed be Canaan; an enslaved servant shall he be to his brothers."

11 And he blessed Shem, and said, "Blessed be the Lord God of Shem, and Canaan shall be his servant.

12 God shall enlarge Japheth, and God shall dwell in the dwelling of Shem, and Canaan shall be his servant."

13 Ham knew that his father had cursed, him, his younger son, and he was displeased that he had cursed him, his son. And Ham parted from his father, he and his sons with him, Cush and Mizraim and Put and Canaan.

14 And he built for himself a city and called its name after the name of his wife Ne'elatama'uk.

15 Japheth saw it, and became envious of his brother, and he too built for himself a city, and he called its name after the name of his wife Adataneses.

16 Shem dwelt with his father Noah, and he built a city close to his father on the mountain, and he too called its name after the name of his wife Sedeqetelebab.

17 These three cities are near Mount Lubar; Sedeqetelebab in front of the mountain on its east; and Na'eltama'uk on the south; Adatan'eses towards the west.

18 These are the sons of Shem, Elam, and Asshur, and Arpachshad who was born two years after the flood, and Lud, and Aram.

19 The sons of Japheth, Gomer, Magog, Madai , Javan, Tubal and Meshech and Tiras, these are the descendants of Noah.

20 In the twenty-eighth jubilee Noah began to direct his sons in the ordinances and commandments, and all the judgments that he knew, and he exhorted his sons to observe righteousness, and to cover the shame of their flesh, and to bless their Creator, and honor father and mother, and love their neighbor, and guard their souls from fornication and uncleanness and all iniquity.

21 Because of these three things came the flood on the earth, namely, the fornication that the Watchers committed against the law of their ordinances when they went whoring after the daughters of men, and took themselves wives of all they chose, and they made the beginning of uncleanness.

22 And they begat sons, the Naphilim (Naphidim), and they were all dissimilar, and they devoured one another, and the Giants killed the Naphil, and the Naphil killed the Eljo, and the Eljo killed mankind, and one man killed one another.

23 Every one committed himself to crime and injustice and to shed much blood, and the earth was filled with sin.

24 After this they sinned against the beasts and birds, and all that moved and walked on the earth, and much blood was shed on the earth, and men continually desired only what was useless and evil.

25 And the Lord destroyed everything from the face of the earth. Because of the wickedness of their deeds, and because of the blood they had shed over all the earth, He destroyed everything. "

26 We were left, I and you, my sons, and everything that entered with us into the ark, and behold I see your works before me that you do not walk in righteousness, for in the path of destruction you have begun to walk, and you are turning one against another, and are envious one of another, and so it comes that you are not in harmony, my sons, each with his brother.

27 For I see the demons have begun their seductions against you and against your children and now I fear on your behalf, that after my death you will shed the blood of men on the earth, and that you, too, will be destroyed from the face of the earth.

28 For whoever sheds man's blood, and who ever eats the blood of any flesh, shall all be destroyed from the earth.

29 There shall be no man left that eats blood, or that sheds the blood of man on the earth, nor shall there be left to him any offspring or descendants living under heaven. Into the abode of the dead shall they go, and into the place of condemnation shall they descend, and into the darkness of the deep shall they all be removed by a violent death.

30 Do not smear blood on yourself or let it remain on you. Out of all the blood there shall be shed and out of all the days in which you have killed any beasts or cattle or whatever flies on the earth you must do a good work to your souls by covering that which has been shed on the face of the earth.

31 You shall not be like him who eats blood, but guard yourselves that none may eat blood before you, cover the blood, for thus have I been commanded to testify to you and your children, together with all flesh.

32 Do not permit the soul (life) to be eaten with the flesh, that your blood, which is your life, may not be required at the hand of any flesh that sheds it on the earth.

33 For the earth will not be clean from the blood that has been shed on it, for only through the blood of him that shed it will the earth be purified throughout all its generations.

34 Now, my children, listen, have judgment and righteousness that you maybe planted in righteousness over the face of the whole earth, and your glory lifted up in the presence of my God, who spared me from the waters of the flood.

35 Look, you will go and build for yourselves cities, and plant in them all the plants that are on the earth, and moreover all fruit-bearing trees.

36 For three years the fruit of everything that is eaten will not be gathered, and in the fourth year its fruit will be accounted holy, offered as first fruit, acceptable before the Most High God, who created heaven and earth and all things.

37 Let them offer in abundance the first of the wine and oil as first-fruits on the altar of the Lord, who receives it, and what is left let the servants of the house of the Lord eat before the altar which receives it.

38 In the fifth year make the release so that you release it in righteousness and uprightness, and you shall be righteous, and all that you plant shall prosper. For this is how Enoch did it, the father of your father commanded Methuselah, his son, and Methuselah commanded his son Lamech, and Lamech commanded me all the things that his fathers commanded him.

39 I also will give you commandment, my sons, as Enoch commanded his son in the first jubilees, while still living, the seventh in his generation, he commanded and testified to his son and to his son's sons until the day of his death.

[Chapter *8*]

1 In the twenty-ninth jubilee, in the beginning of first week, Arpachshad took to himself a wife and her name was Rasu'eja, the daughter of Susan, the daughter of Elam, and she gave birth to a son in the third year in this week, and he called his name Kainam.

2 The son grew, and his father taught him writing, and he went to seek for himself a place where he might seize a city for himself.

3 He found writing which former generations had carved on a rock, and he read what was on it, and he transcribed it and sinned because of it, for it contained the teaching of the Watchers, which they had used to observe the omens of the sun and moon and stars in all the signs of heaven.

4 He wrote it down and said nothing of it, for he was afraid to speak to Noah about it or he would be angry with him because of it.

5 In the thirtieth jubilee, in the second week, in the first year of it, he took to himself a wife, and her name was Melka, the daughter of Madai, the son of Japheth, and in the fourth year he begat a son, and called his name Shelah; for he said, "Truly I have been sent."

6 Shelah grew up and took to himself a wife, and her name was Mu'ak, the daughter of Kesed, his father's brother, in the one and thirtieth jubilee, in the fifth week, in the first year of it.

7 And she gave birth to a son in the fifth year of it, and he called his name Eber, and he took to himself a wife, and her name was Azurad, the daughter of Nebrod, in the thirty-second jubilee, in the seventh week, in the third year of it.

8 In the sixth year of it, she gave birth to a son, and he called his name Peleg, for in the days when he was born the children of Noah began to divide the earth among themselves, for this reason he called his name Peleg.

9 They divided it secretly among themselves, and told it to Noah.

10 In the beginning of the thirty-third jubilee they divided the earth into three parts, for Shem and Ham and Japheth, according to the inheritance of each, in the first year in the first week, when one of us (angels) who had been sent, was with them.

11 He called his sons, and they drew close to him, they and their children, and he divided the earth into the lots, which his three sons were to take in possession, and they reached out their hands, and took the writing out of the arms of Noah, their father.

12 There came out on the writing as Shem's lot the middle of the earth that he should take as an inheritance for himself and for his sons for the generations of eternity. From the middle of the mountain range of Rafa, from the mouth of the water from the river Tina, and his portion goes towards the west through the middle of this river, and it extends until it reaches the water of the abysses, out of which this river goes out and pours its waters into the sea Me'at, and this river flows into the great sea.

13 All that is towards the north is Japheth's, and all that is towards the south belongs to Shem. And it extends until it reaches Karaso, this is in the center of the tongue of land that looks towards the south.

14 His portion extends along the great sea, and it extends in a straight line until it reaches the west of the tongue that looks towards the south, for this sea is named the tongue of the Egyptian Sea.

15 And it turns from here towards the south towards the mouth of the great sea on the shore of its waters, and it extends to the west to Afra, and it extends until it reaches the waters of the river Gihon, and to the south of the waters of Gihon, to the banks of this river.

16 It extends towards the east, until it reaches the Garden of Eden, to the south of it and from the east of the whole land of Eden and of the whole east, it turns to the east and proceeds until it reaches the east of the mountain named Rafa, and it descends to the bank of the mouth of the river Tina.

17 This portion came out by lot for Shem and his sons, that they should possess it forever to his generations forever.

18 Noah rejoiced that this portion came out for Shem and for his sons, and he remembered all that he had spoken with his mouth in prophecy; for he had said, "Blessed be the Lord God of Shem and may the Lord dwell in the dwelling of Shem."

19 He knew that the Garden of Eden is the holy of holies, and the dwelling of the Lord, and Mount Sinai the center of the desert, and Mount Zion which is the center of the navel of the earth, these three were created as holy places facing each other.

20 And he blessed the God of gods, who had put the word of the Lord into his mouth, and the Lord forever.

21 And he knew that a blessed portion and a blessing had come to Shem and his sons and to their generations forever which was the whole land of Eden and the whole land of the Red Sea, and the whole land of the east and India, and on the Red Sea and the mountains of it, and all the land of Bashan, and all the land of Lebanon and the islands of Kaftur, and all the mountains of Sanir and Amana, and the mountains of Asshur in the north, and all the land of Elam, Asshur, and Babel, and Susan and Ma'edai, and all the mountains of Ararat, and all the region beyond the sea, which is beyond the mountains of Asshur towards the north, a blessed and spacious land, and all that is in it is very good.

22 Ham received the second portion, beyond the Gihon towards the south to the right of the Garden, and it extends towards the south and it extends to all the mountains of fire, and it extends towards the west to the sea of 'atel and it extends towards the west until it reaches the sea of Ma'uk which was that sea into which everything that is not destroyed descends.

23 It goes out towards the north to the limits of Gadir, and it goes out to the coast of the waters of the sea to the waters of the great sea until it draws near to the river Gihon, and goes along the river Gihon until it reaches the right of the Garden of Eden.

24 This is the land that came out for Ham as the portion which he was to occupy forever for himself and his sons to their generations forever.

25 Japheth received the third portion beyond the river Tina to the north of the outflow of its waters, and it extends north-easterly to the whole region of Gog, and to all the country east of it.

26 It extends northerly, and it extends to the mountains of Qelt towards the north, and towards the sea of Ma'uk, and it goes out to the east of Gadir as far as the region of the waters of the sea.

27 It extends until it approaches the west of Fara and it returns towards Aferag, and it extends easterly to the waters of the sea of Me'at.

28 It extends to the region of the river Tina in a northeasterly direction until it approaches the boundary of its waters towards the mountain Rafa, and it turns round towards the north.

29 This is the land that came out for Japheth and his sons as the portion of his inheritance that he should possess five great islands, and a great land in the north, for himself and his sons, for their generations forever.

30 But it is cold, and the land of Ham is hot, and the land of Shem is neither hot nor cold, but it is of blended cold and heat.

[Chapter 9]

1 Ham divided among his sons, and the first portion came out for Cush towards the east, and to the west of him for Mizraim, and to the west of him for Put, and to the west of him on the sea for Canaan.

2 Shem also divided among his sons, and the first portion came out for Ham and his sons, to the east of the river Tigris until it approaches the east, the whole land of India, and on the Red Sea on its coast, and the waters of Dedan, and all the mountains of Mebri and Ela, and all the land of Susan and all that is on the side of Pharnak to the Red Sea and the river Tina.

3 Asshur received the second Portion, all the land of Asshur and Nineveh and Shinar and to the border of India, and it ascends and skirts the river.

4 Arpachshad received the third portion, all the land of the region of the Chaldees to the east of the Euphrates, bordering on the Red Sea, and all the waters of the desert close to the tongue of the sea which looks towards Egypt, all the land of Lebanon and Sanir and Amana to the border of the Euphrates.

5 Aram received the fourth portion, all the land of Mesopotamia between the Tigris and the Euphrates to the north of the Chaldees to the border of the mountains of Asshur and the land of Arara.

6 Lud got the fifth portion, the mountains of Asshur and all surrounding to them until it reaches the Great Sea, and until it reaches the east of Asshur his brother.

7 Japheth also divided the land of his inheritance among his sons.

8 The first portion came out for Gomer to the east from the north side to the river Tina, and in the north there came out for Magog all the inner portions of the north until it reaches to the sea of Me'at.

9 Madai received as his portion that he should possess from the west of his two brothers to the islands, and to the coasts of the islands.

10 Javan got the fourth portion, every island and the islands that are towards the border of Lud.

11 For Tubal there came out the fifth portion in the middle of the tongue that approaches towards the border of the portion of Lud to the second tongue, to the region beyond the second tongue to the third tongue.

12 Meshech received the sixth portion, that is the entire region beyond the third tongue until it approaches the east of Gadir.

13 Tiras got the seventh portion, four great islands in the middle of the sea, which reach to the portion of Ham, and the islands of Kamaturi came out by lot for the sons of Arpachshad as his inheritance.

14 Thus the sons of Noah divided to their sons in the presence of Noah their father, and he bound them all by an oath, and invoked a curse on every one that sought to seize any portion which had not fallen to him by his lot.

15 They all said, "so be it; so be it " (amen and amen) for themselves and their sons forever throughout their generations until the day of judgment, on which the Lord God shall judge them with a sword and with fire for all the unclean wickedness of their errors, that they have filled the earth with, which are transgression, uncleanness and fornication and sin.

[Chapter *10*]

1 In the third week of this jubilee the unclean demons began to lead astray the children of the sons of Noah, and to make them sin and to destroy them.

2 The sons of Noah came to Noah their father, and they told him about the demons that were leading astray and blinding and slaying his sons' sons.

3 And he prayed before the Lord his God, and said,

"God of the spirits of all flesh, who have shown mercy to me and have spared me and my sons from the waters of the flood, and have not caused me to die as You did the sons of perdition; For Your grace has been great toward me, and great has been Your mercy to my soul. Let Your grace be lifted up on my sons, and do not let the wicked spirits rule over them or they will destroy them from the earth.

4 But bless me and my sons, so that we may increase and multiply and replenish the earth.

5 You know how Your Watchers, the fathers of these spirits, acted in my day, and as for these spirits which are living, imprison them and hold them fast in the place of condemnation, and let them not bring destruction on the sons of your servant, my God; for these are like cancer and are created in order to destroy.

6 Let them not rule over the spirits of the living; for You alone can exercise dominion over them. And let them not have power over the sons of the righteous from now and forever."

7 And the Lord our God commanded us (angels) to bind all of them.

8 The chief of the spirits, Mastema, came and said, "Lord, Creator, let some of them remain before me, and let them listen to my voice, and do all that I shall say to them; for if some of them are not left to me, I shall not be able to execute the power of my will on the sons of men, for these are for corruption and leading astray before my judgment, for great is the wickedness of the sons of men."

9 He said, "Let one-tenth of them remain before him, and let nine-tenths of them descend into the place of condemnation."

10 He commanded one of us to teach Noah all their medicines, for He knew that they would not walk in uprightness, nor strive in righteousness.

11 We did according to all His words, all the malignant evil ones we bound in the place of condemnation and a tenth part of them we left that they might be subject in the presence of Satan on the earth.

12 We explained to Noah all the medicines of their diseases, together with their seductions, how he might heal them with herbs of the earth.

13 Noah wrote down all things in a book as we instructed him concerning every kind of medicine. Thus the evil spirits were precluded from hurting the sons of Noah.

14 He gave all that he had written to Shem, his eldest son, for he loved him greatly above all his sons.

15 And Noah slept with his fathers, and was buried on Mount Lubar in the land of Ararat.

16 Nine hundred and fifty years he completed in his life, nineteen jubilees and two weeks and five years.

17 In his life on earth he was greater than all the children of men except Enoch because of his righteousness he was perfect. For Enoch's office was ordained for a testimony to the generations of the world, so that he should recount all the deeds of generation to generation, until the day of judgment.

18 In the three and thirtieth jubilee, in the first year in the second week, Peleg took to himself a wife, whose name was

Lomna the daughter of Sina'ar, and she gave birth to a son for him in the fourth year of this week, and he called his name Reu, for he said, "Look the children of men have become evil because the building a city and a tower in the land of Shinar was for an evil purpose."

19 For they departed from the land of Ararat eastward to Shinar, for in his days they built the city and the tower, saying, "Come, let us rise up by the tower into heaven."

20 They began to build, and in the fourth week they made brick with fire, and the bricks served them for stone, and the clay with which they cemented them together was asphalt which comes out of the sea, and out of the fountains of water in the land of Shinar.

21 They built it, forty-three years were they building it. Its breadth was 203 bricks, and the height of a brick was the third of one; its height amounted to 5433 cubits and 2 palms, and the extent of one wall was thirteen times 600 feet and of the other thirty times 600 feet.

22 And the Lord our God said to us, "Look, they are one people, and they begin to do this, and now nothing will be withheld from them. Let us go down and confound their language, that they may not understand one another's speech, and they may be dispersed into cities and nations, and they will not be in agreement together with one purpose until the day of judgment."

23 And the Lord descended, and we descended with him to see the city and the tower that the children of men had built.

24 He confounded their language, and they no longer understood one another's speech, and they then ceased to build the city and the tower.

25 For this reason the whole land of Shinar is called Babel, because the Lord confounded all the language of the children of men there, and from that place they were dispersed into their cities, each according to his language and his nation.

26 Then, the Lord sent a mighty wind against the tower and it fell to the earth, and behold it was between Asshur and Babylon in the land of Shinar, and they called its name "Overthrow."

27 In the fourth week in the first year in the beginning of it in the four and thirtieth jubilee, were they dispersed from the land of Shinar.

28 Ham and his sons went into the land that he was to occupy, which he acquired as his portion in the land of the south.

29 Canaan saw the land of Lebanon to the river of Egypt was very good, and he did not go into the land of his inheritance to the west that is to the sea, and he dwelt in the land of Lebanon, eastward and westward from the border of Jordan and from the border of the sea.

30 Ham, his father, and Cush and Mizraim, his brothers, said to him, "You have settled in a land which is not yours, and which did not fall to us by lot, do not do so. If you do you and your sons will be conquered in the land and be accursed through a war. By war you have settled, and by war will your children fall, and you will be rooted out forever.

31 Do not live in the land of Shem, for to Shem and to his sons did it come by their lot.

32 Cursed are you, and cursed will you be beyond all the sons of Noah, by the curse by which we bound ourselves by an oath in the presence of the holy judge, and in the presence of Noah our father."

33 But he did not listen to them, and settled in the land of Lebanon from Hamath to the border of Egypt, he and his sons until this day. For this reason that land is named Canaan. And Japheth and his sons went towards the sea and settled in the land of their portion, and Madai saw the land of the sea and it did not please him, and he begged Ham and Asshur and Arpachshad, his wife's brother for a portion, and he dwelt in the land of Media, near to his wife's brother until this day.

34 And he called his and his son's dwelling-place, Media, after the name of their father Madai.

[Chapter *11*]

1 In the thirty-fifth jubilee, in the third week, in the first year of it, Reu took to himself a wife, and her name was 'Ora, the daughter of 'Ur, the son of Kesed, and she gave birth to a son, and he called his name Seroh, in the seventh year of this week in this jubilee.

2 The sons of Noah began to war with each other, to take captives and kill each other, and to shed the blood of men on the earth, and to eat blood, and to build strong cities, and walls, and towers, and individuals began to exalt themselves above the nation, and to establish kingdoms, and to go to war, people against people, and nation against nation, and city against city, and all began to do evil, and to acquire arms, and to teach their sons war, and they began to capture cities, and to sell male and female slaves.

3 Ur, the son of Kesed, built the city of Ara of the Chaldees, and called its name after his own name and the name of his father.

4 And they made themselves molten images, and they worshipped the idols and the molten image they had made for themselves, and they began to make graven images and unclean and shadowy presence, and malevolent and malicious spirits assisted and seduced them into committing transgression and uncleanness.

5 Prince Mastema exerted himself to do all this, and he sent out other spirits, which were put under his control, to do all manner of wrong and sin, and all manner of transgression, to corrupt and destroy, and to shed blood on the earth.

6 For this reason he called the name of Seroh, Serug, for every one turned to do all manner of sin and transgression.

7 He grew up, and dwelt in Ur of the Chaldees, near to the father of his wife's mother, and he worshipped idols, and he took to himself a wife in the thirty-sixth jubilee, in the fifth week, in the first year of it, and her name was Melka, the daughter of Kaber, the daughter of his father's brother.

8 She gave birth to Nahor, in the first year of this week, and he grew and dwelt in Ur of the Chaldees, and his father taught him the sciences of the Chaldees to divine and conjure, according to the signs of heaven.

9 In the thirty-seventh jubilee in the sixth week, in the first year of it, he took to himself a wife, and her name was 'Ijaska, the daughter of Nestag of the Chaldees.

10 And she gave birth to Terah in the seventh year of this week.

11 Prince Mastema sent ravens and birds to devour the seed that was sown in the land, in order to destroy the land, and rob the children of men of their labors. Before they could plow in the seed, the ravens picked it from the surface of the ground.

12 This is why he called his name Terah because the ravens and the birds reduced them to destitution and devoured their seed.

13 The years began to be barren, because of the birds, and they devoured all the fruit of the trees from the trees, it was only with great effort that they could harvest a little fruit from the earth in their days.

14 In this thirty-ninth jubilee, in the second week in the first year, Terah took to himself a wife, and her name was 'Edna, the daughter of Abram, the daughter of his father's sister.

15 In the seventh year of this week she gave birth to a son, and he called his name Abram, by the name of the father of his mother, for he had died before his daughter had conceived a son.

16 And the child began to understand the errors of the earth that all went astray after graven images and after uncleanness, and his father taught him writing, and he was two weeks of years old, and he separated himself from his father, that he might not worship idols with him.

17 He began to pray to the Creator of all things that He might spare him from the errors of the children of men, and that his portion should not fall into error after uncleanness and vileness.

18 The time came for the sowing of seed in the land, and they all went out together to protect their seed against the ravens, and Abram went out with those that went, and the child was a lad of fourteen years.

19 A cloud of ravens came to devour the seed, and Abram ran to meet them before they settled on the ground, and cried to them before they settled on the ground to devour the seed, and said, "Descend not, return to the place from where you came," and they began to turn back.

20 And he caused the clouds of ravens to turn back that day seventy times, and of all the ravens throughout all the land where Abram was there settled not so much as one.

21 All who were with him throughout all the land saw him cry out, and all the ravens turn back, and his name became great in all the land of the Chaldees.

22 There came to him this year all those that wished to sow, and he went with them until the time of sowing ceased, and they sowed their land, and that year they brought enough grain home to eat and they were satisfied.

23 In the first year of the fifth week Abram taught those who made implements for oxen, the artificers in wood, and they made a vessel above the ground, facing the frame of the plow, in order to put the seed in it, and the seed fell down from it on the share of the plow, and was hidden in the earth, and they no longer feared the ravens.

24 After this manner they made vessels above the ground on all the frames of the plows, and they sowed and tilled all the land, according as Abram commanded them, and they no longer feared the birds.

[Chapter *12*]

1 In the sixth week, in the seventh year of it, that Abram said to Terah his father, saying, "Father!"

2 He said, "Look, here am I, my son." He said, "What help and profit have we from those idols which you worship, and in the presence of which you bow yourself?

3 For there is no spirit in them. They are dumb forms, and they mislead the heart.

4 Do not worship them, Worship the God of heaven, who causes the rain and the dew to fall on the earth and does everything on the earth, and has created everything by His word, and all life is from His presence.

5 Why do you worship things that have no spirit in them?

For they are the work of men's hands, and you bear them on your shoulders, and you have no help from them, but they are a great cause of shame to those who make them, and they mislead the heart of those who worship them. Do not worship them."

6 His father said to him, "I also know it, my son, but what shall I do with a people who have made me serve them?

7 If I tell them the truth, they will kill me, because their soul clings to them so they worship them and honor them.

8 Keep silent, my son, or they will kill you." And these words he spoke to his two brothers, and they were angry with him and he kept silent.

9 In the fortieth jubilee, in the second week, in the seventh year of it, Abram took to himself a wife, and her name was Sarai, the daughter of his father, and she became his wife.

10 Haran, his brother, took to himself a wife in the third year of the third week, and she gave birth to a son in the seventh year of this week, and he called his name Lot.

11 Nahor, his brother, took to himself a wife.

12 In the sixtieth year of the life of Abram, that is, in the fourth week, in the fourth year of it, Abram arose in the night and burned the house of the idols, and he burned all that was in the house and no man knew it.

13 And they arose and sought to save their gods from the fire.

14 Haran hasted to save them, but the fire flamed over him, and he was burnt in the fire, and he died in Ur of the Chaldees before Terah his father, and they buried him in Ur of the Chaldees.

15 Terah went out from Ur of the Chaldees, he and his sons, to go into the land of Lebanon and into the land of Canaan, and he dwelt in the land of Haran, and Abram dwelt with Terah his father in Haran two weeks of years.

16 In the sixth week, in the fifth year of it, Abram sat up all night on the new moon of the seventh month to observe the stars from the evening to the morning, in order to see what would be the character of the year with regard to the rains, and he was alone as he sat and observed.

17 And a word came into his heart and he said, "All the signs of the stars, and the signs of the moon and of the sun are all in the hand of the Lord. Why do I search them out?

18 If He desires, He causes it to rain, morning and evening, and if He desires, He withholds it, and all things are in his hand."

19 He prayed in the night and said, "My God, God Most High, You alone are my God, and You and Your dominion have I chosen. And You have created all things, and all things that are the work of Your hands.

20 Deliver me from the hands of evil spirits who have dominion over the thoughts of men's hearts, and let them not lead me astray from You, my God. And establish me and my offspring forever so that we do not go astray from now and forever."

21 He said, "Shall I return to Ur of the Chaldees who are trying to find me? Should I return to them? Am I to remain here in this place? The right path is before You. Make it prosper in the hands of your servant that he may fulfill it and that I may not walk in the deceitfulness of my heart, O my God."

22 He stopped speaking and stopped praying, and then the word of the Lord was sent to him through me, saying, "Get out of your country, and from your kindred and from the house of your father and go to a land which I will show you, and I shall make you a great and numerous nation.

23 And I will bless you and I will make your name great,

and you will be blessed in the earth, and in You shall all families of the earth be blessed, and I will bless them that bless you, and curse them that curse you.

24 I will be a God to you and your son, and to your son's son, and to all your offspring, fear not, from now on and to all generations of the earth I am your God."

25 The Lord God said, "Open his mouth and his ears, that he may hear and speak with his mouth, with the language which has been revealed," for it had ceased from the mouths of all the children of men from the day of the overthrow of Babel.

26 And I opened his mouth, and his ears and his lips, and I began to speak with him in Hebrew in the tongue of the creation.

27 He took the books of his fathers, and these were written in Hebrew, and he transcribed them, and he began from then on to study them, and I made known to him that which he could not understand, and he studied them during the six rainy months.

28 In the seventh year of the sixth week he spoke to his father and informed him, that he would leave Haran to go into the land of Canaan to see it and return to him.

29 Terah his father said to him; "Go in peace. May the eternal God make your path straight. And the Lord be with you, and protect you from all evil, and grant to you grace, mercy and favor before those who see you, and may none of the children of men have power over you to harm you. Go in peace.

30 If you see a land pleasant to your eyes to dwell in, then arise and take me with you and take Lot with you, the son of Haran your brother as your own son, the Lord be with you.

31 Nahor your brother leave with me until you return in peace, and we go with you all together."

[Chapter *13*]

1 Abram journeyed from Haran, and he took Sarai, his wife, and Lot, his brother Haran's son and they went to the land of Canaan, and he came into Asshur, and proceeded to Shechem, and dwelt near a tall oak.

2 He saw the land was very pleasant from the border of Hamath to the tall oak.

3 The Lord said to him, "To you and to your offspring I will give this land."

4 He built an altar there, and he offered on it a burnt sacrifice to the Lord, who had appeared to him.

5 He left from that place and went to the mountain Bethel on the west and Ai on the east, and pitched his tent there.

6 He saw the land was very wide and good, and everything grew on it, vines, and figs, and pomegranates, oaks, and ilexes, and turpentine and oil trees, and cedars and cypresses, and date trees, and all trees of the field, and there was water on the mountains.

7 And he blessed the Lord who had led him out of Ur of the Chaldees, and had brought him to this land.

8 In the first year, in the seventh week, on the new moon of the first month, he built an altar on this mountain, and called on the name of the Lord and said, "You, the eternal God, are my God."

9 He offered on the altar a burnt sacrifice to the Lord that He should be with him and not forsake him all the days of his life.

10 He left that place and went toward the south, and he came to Hebron and Hebron was built at that time, and he lived there two years, and he went from that place into the land of the south, to Bealoth, and there was a famine in the land.

11 Abram went into Egypt in the third year of the week, and he dwelt in Egypt five years before his wife was torn away from him.

12 Now, Tanais in Egypt was built seven years after Hebron.

13 When Pharaoh seized Sarai, the wife of Abram the Lord plagued Pharaoh and his house with great plagues because of Sarai, Abram's wife.

14 Abram was celebrated and admired because of his great possessions of sheep, and cattle, and donkeys, and horses, and camels, and menservants, and maidservants, and in silver and gold. Lot and his brother's son were also wealthy.

15 Pharaoh gave back Sarai, the wife of Abram, and he sent him out of the land of Egypt, and he journeyed to the place where he had pitched his tent at the beginning, to the place of the altar, with Ai on the east, and Bethel on the west, and he blessed the Lord his God who had brought him back in peace.

16 In the forty-first jubilee in the third year of the first week, that he returned to this place and offered on it a burnt sacrifice, and called on the name of the Lord, and said, "You, the most high God, are my God forever and ever."

17 In the fourth year of this week Lot parted from him, and Lot lived in Sodom, and the men of Sodom sinned greatly.

18 It grieved him in his heart that his brother's son had parted from him because Abram had no children.

19 After Lot had parted from him, in the fourth year of this week. In that year when Lot was taken captive, the Lord said to Abram, "Lift up your eyes from the place where you are dwelling, northward and southward, and westward and eastward.

20 All the land that you see I will give to you and to your offspring forever, and I will make your offspring as the sand of the sea, though a man may number the dust of the earth, yet your offspring shall not be numbered.

21 Arise, walk through the land in the length of it and the breadth of it, and see it all. To your offspring will I give it." And Abram went to Hebron, and lived there.

22 And in this year came Chedorlaomer, king of Elam, and Amraphel, king of Shinar, and Arioch king of Sellasar, and Tergal, king of nations, and killed the king of Gomorrah, and the king of Sodom fled, and many fell through wounds in the valley of Siddim, by the Salt Sea.

23 They took captive Sodom and Adam and Zeboim, and they took Lot captive, the son of Abram's brother, and all his possessions, and they went to Dan.

24 One who had escaped came and told Abram that his brother's son had been taken captive.

25 And Abram equipped his household servants for Abram, and for his offspring, a tenth of the first-fruits to the Lord, and the Lord ordained it as a law forever that they should give it to the priests who served before Him, that they should possess it forever.

26 There is no limit of days to this law, for He has ordained it for the generations forever that they should give to the Lord the tenth of everything, of the seed and of the wine and of the oil and of the cattle and of the sheep.

27 He gave it to His priests to eat and to drink with joy before Him.

28 The king of Sodom came and bowed down to him, and said, "Our Lord Abram, give to us the souls which you have rescued, but let the booty be yours."

29 And Abram said to him, "I lift up my hands to the Most High God, that from a thread to a shoe-latchet I shall not take anything that is yours so that you could never say, I have made Abram rich, except only what the young men, Aner and Eschol, and Mamre have eaten, and the portion of the men who went with me. These shall take their portion."

[Chapter *14*]

1 After these things, in the fourth year of this week, on the new moon of the third month, the word of the Lord came to Abram in a dream, saying, "Fear not, Abram, I am your defender, and your reward will be very great."

2 He said, "Lord, Lord, what will you give me, seeing I go from here childless, and the son of Maseq, the son of my handmaid, Eliezer of Damascus, he will be my heir, and to me you have given no offspring."

3 He said to him, "This man will not be your heir, but one that will come out of your own bowels. He will be your heir."

4 And He brought him out abroad, and said to him, "Look toward heaven and number the stars if you are able to number them."

5 He looked toward heaven, and beheld the stars. And He said to him, "so shall your offspring be."

6 And he believed in the Lord, and it was counted to him as righteousness.

7 God said to him, "I am the Lord that brought you out of Ur of the Chaldees, to give you the land of the Canaanites to possess it forever, and I will be God to you and to your offspring after you."

8 He said, "Lord, Lord, how shall I know that I shall inherit it?"

9 God said to him, "Take Me a heifer of three years, and a goat of three years, and a sheep of three years, and a turtledove, and a pigeon."

10 And he took all these in the middle of the month and he dwelt at the oak of Mamre, which is near Hebron.

11 He built an altar there, and sacrificed all these. He poured their blood on the altar, and divided them in half, and laid them over against each other, but the birds he did not divide.

12 Birds came down on the pieces, and Abram drove them away, and did not permit the birds to touch them.

13 It happened, when the sun had set, that an ecstasy fell on Abram, and such a horror of great darkness fell on him, and it was said to Abram, "Know of a surety that your offspring shall be a stranger in a land that is not theirs, and they shall be brought into bondage, and afflicted for four hundred years.

14 The nation also to whom they will be in bondage will I judge, and after that they shall come out from that place with many possessions.

15 You will go to your fathers in peace, and be buried in a good old age.

16 But in the fourth generation they shall return here, for the iniquity of the Amorites is not yet full."

17 And he awoke from his sleep, and he arose, and the sun had set; and there was a flame, and a furnace was smoking, and a flame of fire passed between the pieces.

18 On that day the Lord made a covenant with Abram, saying, "To your offspring will I give this land, from the river of Egypt to the great river, the river Euphrates, the Kenites, the Kenizzites, the Kadmonites, the Perizzites, and the Rephaim, the Phakorites, and the Hivites, and the Amorites, and the Canaanites, and the Girgashites, and the Jebusites.

19 The day passed, and Abram offered the pieces, and the birds, and their fruit offerings, and their drink offerings, and the fire devoured them.

20 On that day we made a covenant with Abram, in the same way we had covenanted with Noah in this month; and Abram renewed the festival and laws for himself forever.

21 Abram rejoiced, and made all these things known to Sarai his wife. He believed that he would have offspring, but she did not bear.

22 Sarai advised her husband Abram, and said to him, "Go in to Hagar, my Egyptian maid, it may be that I shall build up offspring to you by her."

23 Abram listened to the voice of Sarai his wife, and said to her, "Do so." And Sarai took Hagar, her maid, the Egyptian, and gave her to Abram, her husband, to be his wife.

24 He went in to her, and she conceived and gave birth to a son, and he called his name Ishmael, in the fifth year of this week; and this was the eighty-sixth year in the life of Abram.

[Chapter *15*]

1 In the fifth year of the fourth week of this jubilee, in the third month, in the middle of the month, Abram celebrated the feast of the first-fruits of the grain harvest.

2 And he made new offerings on the altar, the first-fruits of the produce to the Lord, a heifer, and a goat, and a sheep on the altar as a burnt sacrifice to the Lord; their fruit offerings and their drink offerings he offered on the altar with frankincense.

3 The Lord appeared to Abram, and said to him, "I am God Almighty. Examine yourself and demonstrate yourself before me and be perfect.

4 I will make My covenant between Me and you, and I will multiply you greatly."

5 Abram fell on his face, and God talked with him, and said, "My law is with you, and you will be the father of many nations.

6 Neither shall your name any more be called Abram, but your name from now on, even forever, shall be Abraham.

7 For I have made you the father of many nations.

8 I will make you very great, and I will make you into nations, and kings shall come forth from you.

9 I shall establish My covenant between Me and you, and your offspring after you, throughout their generations, for an eternal covenant, so that I may be a God to you, and to your offspring after you.

10 You may possess the land where you have been a sojourner, the land of Canaan, and you will possess it forever, and I will be their God."

11 The Lord said to Abraham, "Keep my covenant, you and your offspring after you, and circumcise every male among you, and circumcise your foreskins, and it shall be a token of an eternal covenant between Me and you.

12 And the eighth day you shall circumcise the child, every male throughout your generations, him that is born in the house, or whom you have bought with money from any stranger, whom you have acquired who is not of your offspring.

13 He that is born in your house shall surely be circumcised, and those whom you have bought with money shall be circumcised, and My covenant shall be in your flesh for an eternal ordinance.

14 The uncircumcised male who is not circumcised in the flesh of his foreskin on the eighth day, that soul shall be cut off from his people, for he has broken My covenant."

15 God said to Abraham, "As for Sarai your wife, her name shall no more be called Sarai, but Sarah shall be her name.

16 I will bless her, and give you a son by her, and I will bless him, and he shall become a nation, and kings of nations shall proceed from him."

17 Abraham fell on his face, and rejoiced, and said in his heart, "Shall a son be born to him that is a hundred years old, and shall Sarah, who is ninety years old, bring forth?"

18 Abraham said to God, "Oh, that Ishmael might live before you!"

19 God said, "Yea, and Sarah also shall bear you a son, and you will call his name Isaac, and I will establish My covenant with him, an everlasting covenant, and for his offspring after him.

20 And as for Ishmael also have I heard you, and behold I will bless him, and make him great, and multiply him greatly, and he shall beget twelve princes, and I will make him a great nation.

21 But My covenant will I establish with Isaac, whom Sarah shall bear to you this time next year."

22 God ceased speaking with him, and God went up from Abraham.

23 Abraham did according as God had said to him, and he took Ishmael his son, and all that were born in his house, and whom he had bought with his money, every male in his house, and circumcised the flesh of their foreskin.

24 On that same day was Abraham circumcised, and all the men of his house, and all those whom he had bought with money from the children of the stranger were circumcised with him.

25 This law is for all the generations forever, and there is no variance of days, and no omission of one day out of the eight days, for it is an eternal law, ordained and written on the heavenly tablets.

26 Every one that is born, the flesh of whose foreskin is not circumcised on the eighth day, does not belong to the children of the covenant which the Lord made with Abraham, but instead they belong to the children of destruction; nor is there any other sign on him that he is the Lord's, but he is destined to be destroyed and killed from the earth, and to be rooted out of the earth, for he has broken the covenant of the Lord our God.

27 All the angels of the presence (of the Lord) and all the angels of sanctification have been created already circumcised from the day of their creation, and before the angels of the presence (of the Lord) and the angels of sanctification He has sanctified Israel, that they should be with Him and with His holy angels.

28 Command the children of Israel and let them observe the sign of this covenant for their generations as an eternal law, and they will not be rooted out of the land.

29 For the command is ordained for a covenant, that they should observe it forever among all the children of Israel.

30 For Ishmael and his sons and his brothers, and Esau, the Lord did not cause them to come to Him, and he did not choose them. Although they are the children of Abraham, He knew them, but He chose Israel to be His people.

31 He sanctified them, and gathered them from among all the children of men; for there are many nations and many peoples, and all are His, and over all nations He has placed spirits in authority to lead them astray from Him.

32 But over Israel He did not appoint any angel or spirit, for He alone is their ruler, and He will preserve them and require them at the hand of His angels and His spirits, and at the hand of all His powers in order that He may preserve them and bless them, that they may be His and He may be theirs from now on forever.

33 I announce to you that the children of Israel will not keep true to this law, and they will not circumcise their sons according to all this law; for in the flesh of their circumcision they will omit this circumcision of their sons, and all of the sons of Beliar will leave their sons uncircumcised as they were born.

34 There will be great wrath from the Lord against the children of Israel because they have forsaken His covenant and turned aside from His word, and provoked (God) and blasphemed, because they do not observe the ordinance of this law; for they have treated their genitalia like the Gentiles, so that they may be removed and rooted out of the land. And there will no more be pardon or forgiveness to them for all the sin of this eternal error.

[Chapter *16*]

1 On the new moon of the fourth month we appeared to Abraham, at the oak of Mamre, and we talked with him, and we announced to him that Sarah, his wife, would give him a son.

2 And Sarah laughed, for she heard that we had spoken these words to Abraham. We warned her, and she became afraid, and denied that she had laughed because of the words.

3 We told her the name of her son, as his name is ordained and written in the heavenly tablets and it is Isaac.

4 We told her that when we returned to her at a set time, she would have conceived a son.

5 In this month the Lord executed his judgments on Sodom, and Gomorrah, and Zeboim, and all the region of the Jordan, and He burned them with fire and brimstone, and destroyed them and they are destroyed until this day, because of all their works. They are wicked and vast sinners, and they defile themselves and commit fornication in their flesh, and work uncleanness on the earth as I have told you.

6 In like manner, God will execute judgment on the places where they have done similar to the uncleanness of the Sodomites, and they will suffer a judgment like that of Sodom.

7 But for Lot, we made an exception, for God remembered Abraham, and sent him out from the place of the overthrow.

8 And he and his daughters committed sin on the earth, such as had not been on the earth since the days of Adam until his time, for the man had sex with his daughters.

9 It was commanded and engraved concerning all his offspring, on the heavenly tablets, to remove them and root them out, and to execute judgment on them like the judgment of Sodom, and to leave no offspring of that man on earth on the day of condemnation.

10 In this month Abraham moved from Hebron, and departed and lived between Kadesh and Shur in the mountains of Gerar.

11 In the middle of the fifth month he moved from that place, and lived at the Well of the Oath.

12 In the middle of the sixth month the Lord visited Sarah and did to her as He had spoken and she conceived.

13 And she gave birth to a son in the third month. In the middle of the month, at the time of which the Lord had spoken to Abraham, on the festival of the first-fruits of the harvest, Isaac was born.

14 Abraham circumcised his son on the eighth day, he was the first that was circumcised according to the covenant that is ordained forever.

15 In the sixth year of the fourth week we came to Abraham at the Well of the Oath, and we appeared to him.

16 We returned in the seventh month, and found Sarah with child before us and we blessed him, and we announced to him all the things that had been decreed concerning him, so that he should not die until he should beget six more sons and saw them before he died.

17 But in Isaac should his name and offspring be called, and that all the offspring of his sons should be Gentiles, and be counted with the Gentiles; but from the sons of Isaac one should become a holy offspring, and should not be counted among the Gentiles.

18 For he should become the portion (dowry) of the Most High, and all his offspring had fallen into the possession of God, that they should be to the Lord a people for His possession above all nations and that they should become a kingdom and priests and a holy nation.

19 We went our way, and we announced to Sarah all that we had told him, and they both rejoiced with very great joy.

20 He built there an altar to the Lord who had delivered him, and who was causing him to rejoice in the land of his sojourning, and he celebrated a festival of joy in this month for seven days, near the altar which he had built at the Well of the Oath.

21 He built tents for himself and for his servants on this festival, and he was the first to celebrate the feast of tabernacles on the earth.

22 During these seven days he brought a burnt offering to the Lord each day to the altar consisting of two oxen, two rams, seven sheep, one male goat, for a sin offering that he might atone thereby for himself and for his offspring.

23 As an offering of thanks he brought, seven rams, seven kids, seven sheep, and seven male goats, and their fruit offerings and their drink offerings; and he burnt all the fat of it on the altar, a chosen offering to the Lord for a sweet smelling odor.

24 Morning and evening he burnt fragrant substances, frankincense and incense, and sweet spice, and nard, and myrrh, and spice, and aromatic plants; all these seven he offered, crushed, mixed together in equal parts and pure.

25 And he celebrated this feast during seven days, rejoicing with all his heart and with all his soul, he and all those who were in his house, and there was no stranger with him, nor any that was uncircumcised.

26 He blessed his Creator who had created him in his generation, for He had created him according to His good pleasure. God knew and perceived that from him would arise the plant of righteousness for the eternal generations, and from him a holy offspring, so that it should become like Him who had made all things.

27 He blessed and rejoiced, and he called the name of this festival the festival of the Lord, a joy acceptable to the Most High God.

28 And we blessed him forever, and all his offspring after him throughout all the generations of the earth, because he celebrated this festival in its season, according to the testimony of the heavenly tablets.

29 For this reason it is ordained on the heavenly tablets concerning Israel, that they shall celebrate the feast of tabernacles seven days with joy, in the seventh month, acceptable before the Lord as a statute forever throughout their generations every year.

30 To this there is no limit of days; for it is ordained forever regarding Israel that they should celebrate it and dwell in tents, and set wreaths on their heads, and take leafy boughs, and willows from the brook.

31Abraham took branches of palm trees, and the fruit of good and pleasing trees, and every day going round the altar with the branches seven times a day in the morning, he praised and gave thanks to his God for all things in joy.

[Chapter *17*]

1 In the first year of the fifth week Isaac was weaned in this jubilee, and Abraham made a great banquet in the third month, on the day his son Isaac was weaned.

2 Ishmael, the son of Hagar, the Egyptian, was in front of Abraham, his father, in his place, and Abraham rejoiced and blessed God because he had seen his sons and had not died childless.

3 He remembered the words which He had spoken to him on the day that Lot had departed from him, and he rejoiced because the Lord had given him offspring on the earth to inherit the earth, and he blessed with all his mouth the Creator of all things.

4 Sarah saw Ishmael playing and dancing, and Abraham rejoicing with great joy, and she became jealous of Ishmael and said to Abraham, "Throw out this bondwoman and her son. The son of this bondwoman will not be heir with my son, Isaac."

5 And the situation was troubling to Abraham, because of his maidservant and because of his son, because he did not want to drive them from him.

6 God said to Abraham "Let it not be troubling in your sight, because of the child and because of the bondwoman. Listen to Sarah and to all her words and do them, for in Isaac shall your name and offspring be called.

7 But as for the son of this bondwoman I will make him a great nation, because he is of your offspring."

8 Abraham got up early in the morning, and took bread and a bottle of water, and placed them on the shoulders of Hagar and the child, and sent her away.

9 And she departed and wandered in the wilderness of Beersheba, and the water in the bottle was spent, and the child was thirsty, and was not able to go on, and fell down.

10 His mother took him and laid him under an olive tree, and went and sat her down over away from him at the distance of a bow-shot; for she said, "Let me not see the death of my child," and she sat and wept.

11 An angel of God, one of the holy ones, said to her, "Why do you weep, Hagar? Stand. Take the child, and hold him in your hand, for God has heard your voice, and has seen the child."

12 She opened her eyes, and she saw a well of water, and she went and filled her bottle with water, and she gave her child a drink, and she arose and went towards the wilderness of Paran.

13 And the child grew and became an archer, and God was with him, and his mother took him a wife from among the daughters of Egypt.

14 She (the wife) gave birth to a son, and he called his name Nebaioth; for she said, "The Lord was close to me when I called on him."

15 In the seventh week, in the first year of it, in the first month in this jubilee, on the twelfth of this month, there were voices in heaven regarding Abraham, that he was faithful in all that He told him, and that he loved the Lord, and that in every affliction he was faithful.

16 Prince Mastema came and said before God, "Look, Abraham loves Isaac his son, and he delights in him above all things, tell him to offer him as a burnt-offering on the altar, and You will see if he will do this command, and You will know if he is faithful in everyway that You test him.

17 The Lord knew that Abraham was faithful throughout all his afflictions, for He had tried him through his country and with famine, and had tried him with the wealth of kings, and had tried him again through his wife, when she was torn from him, and with circumcision; and had tried him through Ishmael and Hagar, his maid-servant, when he sent them away.

18 In everything that He had tried him, he was found faithful, and his soul was not impatient, and he was not slow to act, because he was faithful and a lover of the Lord.

[Chapter *18*]

1 God said to him, "Abraham. Abraham." and he said, "Look, here am I."

2 He said, "Take your beloved son, Isaac, whom you love, and go to the high country, and offer him on one of the mountains which I will point out to you."

3 He got early in the morning and saddled his donkey, and took two young men with him, and Isaac his son, and split the wood of the burnt offering, and he went to the place on the third day, and he saw the place afar off.

4 He came to a well of water (near Mount Moriah), and he said to his young men, "You stay here with the donkey, and I and the lad shall go yonder, and when we have worshipped we shall come back to you."

5 He took the wood of the burnt-offering and laid it on Isaac his son, and he took the fire and the knife, and they went both of them together to that place.

6 Isaac said to his father, "Father" and he said, "Here am I, my son." He said to him, "Look, we have the fire, and the knife, and the wood, but where is the sheep for the burnt-offering, father?"

7 He said, "God will provide for himself a sheep for a burnt-offering, my son." And he neared the place of the mountain of God.

8 He built an altar, and he placed the wood on the altar, and bound Isaac his son, and placed him on the wood that was on the altar, and stretched out his hand to take the knife to kill Isaac, his son.

9 I stood in the presence of him, and before prince Mastema, (and the holy angels stood and wept over the altar as prince Mastema and his angels rejoiced and said "Isaac will be destroyed and we will see if Abraham is faithful), and the Lord said, "Command him not to lay his hand on the lad, nor to do anything to him, for I have shown that he fears the Lord."

10 I called to him from heaven, and said to him, "Abraham, Abraham." and he was terrified and said, "Here am I."

11 I said to him, "Lay not your hand on the lad, neither do anything to him; for now I have shown that you fear the Lord, and have not withheld your son, your first-born son, from me."

12 Prince Mastema was put to shame (and was bound by the angels); and Abraham lifted up his eyes and looked and saw a ram caught by his horns, and Abraham went and took the ram and offered it as a burnt-offering in place of his son.

13 Abraham called that place "The Lord has seen," so that it is said the Lord has seen. This is Mount Zion.

14 The Lord called Abraham by his name a second time from heaven, as he caused us to appear to speak to him in the name of the Lord.

15 He said, "By Myself have I sworn," said the Lord, "Because you have done this thing, and have not withheld your son, your beloved son, from Me, that in blessing I will bless you, and in multiplying I will multiply your offspring as the stars of heaven, and as the sand which is on the seashore.

16 Your offspring shall inherit the cities of their enemies, and in your offspring shall all nations of the earth be blessed. Because you have obeyed My voice, and I have shown to all that you are faithful to Me in all that I have said to you, "Go in peace."

17 Abraham went back to his young men, and they stood and went back together to Beersheba, and Abraham lived by the Well of the Oath.

18 And he celebrated this festival every year, seven days with joy, and he called it the festival of the Lord according to the seven days during which he went and returned in peace.

19 Accordingly, it has been ordained and written on the heavenly tablets regarding Israel and its children that they should observe this festival seven days with the joy of festival.

[Chapter *19*]

1 In the first year of the first week in the forty-second jubilee, Abraham returned and lived across from Hebron, in Kirjath Arba for two weeks of years.

2 In the first year of the third week of this jubilee the days of the life of Sarah were completed, and she died in Hebron.

3 Abraham went to mourn over her and bury her, and we tested him to see if his spirit was patient and he had neither anger nor contempt in the words of his mouth, and he was found patient in this and was not disturbed.

4 In patience of spirit he discussed with the children of Heth that they should give him a place in which to bury his dead.

5 And the Lord gave him grace before all who saw him, and he asked the sons of Heth in gentleness, and they gave him the land of the double cave over beside Mamre, that is Hebron, for four hundred pieces of silver.

6 They said to him, "We shall give it to you for nothing," but he would not take it from them for nothing, for he gave the price of the place and paid the money in full. And he bowed down before them twice, and after this he buried his dead in the double cave.

7 All the days of the life of Sarah were one hundred and twenty-seven years, that is, two jubilees and four weeks and one year, these are the days of the years of the life of Sarah.

8 This is the tenth trial with which Abraham was tested, and he was found faithful and patient in spirit.

9 He did not say a single word regarding the rumor in the land of how God had said that He would give it to him and to his offspring after him, but instead he begged for a place there to bury his dead. Because he was found faithful, it was recorded on the heavenly tablets that he was the friend of God.

10 In the fourth year of it (this jubilee) he took a wife for his son Isaac and her name was Rebecca the daughter of Bethuel, the son of Nahor, the brother of Abraham the sister of Laban and daughter of Bethuel; and Bethuel was the son of Melca, who was the wife of Nahor, the brother of Abraham.

11 Abraham took to himself a third wife from among the daughters of his household servants, for Hagar had died before Sarah, and her name was Keturah,. And she gave birth to six sons, Zimram, and Jokshan, and Medan, and Midian, and Ishbak, and Shuah, in the two weeks of years.

12 In the sixth week, in the second year of it, Rebecca gave birth to two sons of Isaac, Jacob and Esau.

13 And Jacob had no beard and was a straight and tall man who dwelt in tents, and Esau was a powerful a man of the field, and was hairy.

14 The youths grew, and Jacob learned to write, but Esau did not learn, for he was a man of the field and a hunter, and he learned war, and all his deeds were fierce.

15 Abraham loved Jacob, but Isaac loved Esau.

16 And Abraham saw the deeds of Esau, and he knew that in Jacob should his name and offspring be called. He called Rebecca and gave commandment regarding Jacob, for he knew that she too loved Jacob much more than Esau.

17 He said to her, "My daughter, watch over my son Jacob, for he shall take my place on the earth. He shall be a blessing throughout the children of men and for the glory of all the offspring of Shem.

18 I know that the Lord will choose him to be a people (nation) and a possession to Himself, above all peoples that are on the face of the earth.

19 Isaac, my son, loves Esau more than Jacob, but I see that you truly love Jacob.

20 Add still further to your kindness to him, and regard him in love, for he shall be a blessing to us on the earth from now on to all generations of the earth.

21 Let your hands be strong and let your heart rejoice in your son Jacob, for I have loved him far beyond all my sons. He shall be blessed forever, and his offspring shall fill the whole earth.

22 If a man can number the sand of the earth, his offspring also shall be numbered.

23 And all the blessings with which the Lord has blessed me and my offspring shall belong to Jacob and his offspring always.

24 In his offspring shall my name be blessed, and the name of my fathers, Shem, Noah, Enoch, Mahalalel, Enos, Seth, and Adam. And these shall serve to lay the foundations of the heaven, and to strengthen the earth, and to renew all the stars and planets which are in the sky.

27 He called Jacob and kissed him in front of Rebecca, his mother, and blessed him, and said, "Jacob, my beloved son, whom my soul loves, may God bless you from above the sky, and may He give you all the blessings with which He blessed Adam, Enoch, Noah, and Shem; and all the things of which He told me, and all the things which He promised to give me, may He cause to be yours and your offspring forever, according to the days of heaven above the earth.

28 And the Spirits of Mastema shall not rule over you or over your offspring or turn you from the Lord, who is your God from now on forever.

29 May the Lord God be a father to you and may you be like His first-born son, and to the people always. Go in peace, my son."

30 And they both went out together from Abraham.

31 Rebecca loved Jacob, with all her heart and with all her soul, very much more than Esau, but Isaac loved Esau much more than Jacob.

[Chapter *20*]

1 In the forty-second jubilee, in the first year of the seventh week, Abraham called Ishmael, and his twelve sons, and Isaac and his two sons, and the six sons of Keturah, and their sons.

2 And he commanded them that they should observe the way of the Lord, that they should work righteousness, and love each his neighbor, and act in this manner among all men, that they should each walk with regard to the ways of the Lord to do judgment and righteousness on the earth.

3 He also commanded them that they should circumcise their sons, according to the covenant, which God had made with them, and not deviate to the right or the left of all the paths which the Lord had commanded us, and that we should keep ourselves from all fornication and uncleanness.

4 He said, "If any woman or maid commits fornication among you, burn her with fire. And do not let them commit fornication with her with their eyes or their heart; and do not let them take to themselves wives from the daughters of Canaan, because the offspring of Canaan will be rooted out of the land."

5 He told them about the judgment on the giants, and the judgment on the Sodomites, how they had been judged because of their wickedness, and had died because of their fornication and uncleanness, and corruption through fornication together.

6 He said, "Guard yourselves from all fornication and uncleanness, and from all pollution of sin, or you will make our name a curse, and your whole life a shame, and all your sons to be destroyed by the sword, and you will become accursed like Sodom, and all that is left of you shall be as the sons of Gomorrah.

7 I implore you, my sons, love the God of heaven and cling to all His commandments.

8 Do not walk after their idols and after their ways of uncleanness, and do not make yourselves molten or graven gods. They are empty, and there is no spirit in them, for they are work of men's hands, and all who trust in them, trust in nothing.

9 Do not serve them, nor worship them, but serve the most high God, and worship Him continually, and hope for His presence always, and work uprightness and righteousness before Him, that He may have pleasure in you and grant you His mercy, and send rain on you morning and evening, and bless all your works which you have performed on the earth, and bless your bread and your water, and bless the fruit of your womb and the fruit of your land, and the herds of your cattle, and the flocks of your sheep.

10 You will be for a blessing on the earth, and all nations of the earth will desire you, and bless your sons in my name, that they may be blessed as I am."

11 He gave to Ishmael and to his sons, and to the sons of Keturah, gifts, and sent them away from Isaac his son, and he gave everything to Isaac his son.

12 Ishmael and his sons, and the sons of Keturah and their sons, went together and settled from Paran to the border of Babylon in all the land that is toward the East facing the desert.

13 These mingled (intermarried) with each other, and their names were called Arabs, and Ishmaelites.

[Chapter *21*]

1 In the sixth year of the seventh week of this jubilee Abraham called Isaac his son, and commanded him, saying, "I have become old. I do not know the day of my death but I am full of my days.

2 I am one hundred and seventy-five years old, and throughout all the days of my life I have remembered the Lord, and sought with all my heart to do His will, and to walk uprightly in all His ways.

3 My soul has hated idols. I have given my heart and spirit to the observance of the will of Him who created me.

4 For He is the living God, and He is holy and faithful, and He is righteous beyond all, and He is no respecter of men or of their gifts, for God is righteous, and executes judgment on all those who transgress His commandments and despise His covenant.

5 My son, observe His commandments and His law and His judgments, and do not walk after the abominations and after the graven images and after the molten images.

6 And eat no blood at all of animals or cattle, or of any bird that flies in the heaven.

7 If you kill a sacrificial animal as an acceptable peace offering, kill it, and pour out its blood on the altar. Place all the fat of the offering on the altar with fine flour and the meat offering mingled with oil with its drink offering. Place them all together on the altar of burnt offering. It is a sweet odor before the Lord.

8 You will offer the fat of the sacrifice of thanks offerings on the fire which is on the altar, and the fat which is on the belly, and all the fat on the inside, behind the two kidneys, and all the fat that is on them, and lobes of the liver you will remove, together with the kidneys.

9 Offer all these for a sweet odor acceptable before the Lord, with its meat-offering and with its drink-offering, and the bread of the offering to the Lord.

10 Eat its meat on that day and on the second day, but do not let the sun go down on it until it is eaten. Let nothing be left over for the third day, for it is not acceptable. Let it no longer be eaten, and all who eat of it will bring sin on themselves, for thus I have found it written in the books of my forefathers, and in the words of Enoch, and in the words of Noah.

11 On all your offerings you will scatter salt, and do not let the salt of the covenant be lacking in all your offerings before the Lord.

12 As regards the wood of the sacrifices, beware to bring only these and no other wood to the altar in addition to these, cypress, bay, almond, fir, pine, cedar, savin, fig, olive, myrrh, laurel, and aspalathus.

13 Of these kinds of wood lay on the altar under the sacrifice, such as have been tested as to their appearance, and do not lay on it any split or dark wood, but only hard and clean wood, without fault, a healthy, new growth. Do not lay old wood on it, because there is no longer fragrance in it as before.

14 Besides these kinds of wood there is none other that you will place on the altar, for the fragrance is dispersed, and the smell of its fragrance will not go up to heaven.

15 Observe this commandment and do it, my son, that you may be upright in all your deeds.

16 Be clean in your body at all times. Wash yourself with water before you approach to offer on the altar. Wash your hands and your feet before you draw near to the altar, and when you are done sacrificing, wash your hands and feet again.

17 Let no blood appear on you or on your clothes. Be on your guard against blood, my son. Be on your guard continually and cover it with dust.

18 Do not eat any blood for it is the soul. Eat no blood whatsoever.

19 Take no payment for shedding the blood of man, or it will cause it to be shed without fear of punishment, without judgment. It is the blood that is shed that causes the earth to sin, and the earth cannot be cleansed from the blood of man except by the blood of he who shed it.

20 Take no present or gift for the blood of man, blood for blood, that you may be accepted before the Lord, the Most High God. He is the defense of the good, so that you may be preserved from all evil, and that He may withhold you from every kind of death.

21 I see, my son, all the works of the children of men are sin and wickedness, and all their deeds are uncleanness and an abomination and a pollution, and there is no righteousness in them.

22 Beware, or you will walk in their ways and tread in their paths, and commit a sin worthy of death before the Most High God. He will hide His face from you and give you back into the hands of your transgression, and root you out of the land, and your offspring likewise from under heaven, and your name and your offspring shall perish from the whole earth.

23 Turn away from all their deeds and all their uncleanness, and observe the laws of the Most High God, and do His will and be upright in all things.

24 If you do this, He will bless you in all your deeds, and will raise up from you a plant of righteousness through all the earth, throughout all generations of the earth, and my name and your name shall not be forgotten under heaven forever.

25 Go, my son in peace. May the Most High God, my God and your God, strengthen you to do His will, and may He bless all your offspring and the remainder of your offspring for the generations forever, with all righteous blessings, that you may be a blessing on all the earth."

26 And he went out from him rejoicing.

[Chapter *22*]

1 In the first week in the forty-fourth jubilee, in the second year, that is, the year in which Abraham died, Isaac and Ishmael came from the Well of the Oath to celebrate the feast of weeks which is the feast of the first-fruits of the harvest to Abraham, their father, and Abraham rejoiced because his two sons had come.

2 Isaac had many possessions in Beersheba, and Isaac desired to go and see his possessions and to return to his father.

3 In those days Ishmael came to see his father, and they both came together, and Isaac offered a sacrifice for a burnt offering, and presented it on the altar of his father that he had made in Hebron.

4 He offered a thanks offering and made a feast of joy in the presence of Ishmael, his brother, and Rebecca made new cakes from the new grain, and gave them to Jacob, her son, to take them to Abraham, his father, from the first-fruits of the land, that he might eat and bless the Creator of all things before he died.

5 Isaac, also, sent Jacob to Abraham with an offering of his best for thanks so that he might eat and drink.

6 He ate and drank, and blessed the Most High God, who has created heaven and earth, who has made all the fat things of the earth, and given them to the children of men that they might eat and drink and bless their Creator.

7 "And now I give thanks to You, my God, because you have caused me to see this day, behold, I am one hundred three score and fifteen years, an old man and full of days, and all my days have been peace to me.

8 The sword of the adversary has not overcome me in all that You have given me and my children all the days of my life until this day.

9 My God, may Your mercy and Your peace be on Your servant, and on the offspring of his sons, that they may be to You a chosen nation and an inheritance from among all the nations of the earth from now on to all the days of the generations of the earth, to all the ages."

10 He called Jacob and said, "My son Jacob, may the God of all bless you and strengthen you to do righteousness, and His will before Him, and may He choose you and your offspring that you may become a people for His inheritance according to His will always.

11 My son, Jacob, draw near and kiss me." And he drew near and kissed him, and he said, "Blessed be my son Jacob and all the sons of God Most High, to all the ages. May God give to you an offspring of righteousness; and some of your sons may He sanctify throughout the whole earth. May nations serve you, and all the nations bow themselves before your offspring.

12 Be strong in the presence of men, and exercise authority over all the offspring of Seth. Then your ways and the ways of your sons will be justified, so that they shall become a holy nation.

13 May the Most High God give you all the blessings with which He has blessed me and He blessed Noah and Adam. May they rest on the sacred head of your offspring from generation to generation forever.

14 May He cleanse you from all unrighteousness and impurity so that you may be forgiven all the transgressions, which you have committed ignorantly. May He strengthen you, and bless you.

15 May you inherit the whole earth, and may He renew His covenant with you so that you may be to Him a nation for His inheritance for all the ages, and so that He may be to you and to your offspring a God in truth and righteousness throughout all the days of the earth.

16 My son Jacob, remember my words. Observe the commandments of Abraham, your father, separate yourself from the nations (gentiles), and do not eat with them. Do not emulate their works, and do not associate with them because their works are unclean, and all their ways are a pollution and an abomination and uncleanness.

17 They offer their sacrifices to the dead and they worship evil spirits, and they eat over the graves, and all their works are empty and nothingness.

18 They have no heart to understand and their eyes do not see what their works are, and how they go astray by saying to a piece of wood, "You are my God," and to a stone, "You are my Lord and you are my deliverer," because the stone and wood have no heart.

19 And as for you, my son Jacob, may the Most High God help you and the God of heaven bless you and remove you from their uncleanness and from all their error.

20 Jacob, be warned. Do not take a wife from any offspring of the daughters of Canaan, for all his offspring are to be rooted out of the earth.

21 Because of the transgression of Ham, Canaan erred, and all his offspring shall be destroyed from the earth including any remnant of it, and none springing from him shall exist except on the day of judgment.

22 And as for all the worshippers of idols and the profane, there shall be no hope for them in the land of the living, and no one on earth will remember them, for they shall descend into the abode of the dead, and they shall go into the place of condemnation. As the children of Sodom were taken away from the earth, so will all those who worship idols be taken away.

23 Fear not, my son Jacob. Be not dismayed, son of Abraham. May the Most High God preserve you from destruction, and may He deliver you from all the paths of error.

24 This house have I built for myself that I might put my name on it in the earth. It is given to you and to your offspring forever, and it will be named the house of Abraham. It is given to you and your offspring forever, for you will build my house and establish my name before God forever. Your offspring and your name will stand throughout all generations of the earth."

25 He ceased commanding him and blessing him.

26 The two lay together on one bed, and Jacob slept in the embracing arms of Abraham, his father's father, and he kissed him seven times, and his affection and his heart rejoiced over him.

27 He blessed him with all his heart and said, "The Most High God, the God of all, and Creator of all, who brought me out from Ur of the Chaldees that He might give me this land to inherit forever, that I might establish a holy offspring.

28 Blessed be the Most High forever."

29 And he blessed Jacob and said, "May Your grace and Your mercy be lift up on my son, over whom I rejoice with all my heart and my affection and on his offspring always.

30 Do not forsake him, nor diminish him from now to the days of eternity, and may Your eyes be opened on him and on his offspring, that You may preserve him, and bless him, and may sanctify him as a nation for Your inheritance. Bless him with all Your blessings from now to all the days of eternity, and renew Your covenant and Your grace with him and with his offspring according to all Your good pleasure to all the generations of the earth."

[Chapter 23]

1 He placed Jacob's two fingers on his eyes, and he blessed the God of gods, and he covered his face and stretched out his feet and slept the sleep of eternity, and was gathered to his fathers.

2 In spite of all this, Jacob was lying in his embracing arms, and knew not that Abraham, his father's father, was dead.

3 Jacob awoke from his sleep, and realized Abraham was cold as ice, and he said, "Father, father," but there was no answer, and he knew that he was dead.

4 He arose from his embracing arms and ran and told Rebecca, his mother, and Rebecca went to Isaac in the night, and told him and they went together, and Jacob with them, and a lamp was in his hand, and when they had gone in they found Abraham lying dead.

5 Isaac fell on the face of his father and wept and kissed him.

6 Ishmael, his son, heard the voices in the house of Abraham, and he arose, and went to Abraham his father, and wept over Abraham his father, he and all the house of Abraham, and they wept greatly.

7 His sons, Isaac and Ishmael, buried him in the double cave, near Sarah his wife, and all the men of his house, and Isaac and Ishmael, and all their sons, and all the sons of Keturah in their places wept for him forty days and then the days of weeping for Abraham were ended.

8 He lived three jubilees and four weeks of years, one hundred and seventy-five years, and completed the days of his life, being old and full of days.

9 For the days of the lives of their forefathers were nineteen jubilees; and after the Flood they began to grow less than nineteen jubilees, and to decrease in jubilees, and to grow old quickly, and to be full of their days because of the many types of hardships and the wickedness of their ways, with the exception of Abraham.

10 For Abraham was perfect in all his deeds with the Lord, and well-pleasing in righteousness all the days of his life. Yet, he did not complete four jubilees in his life, when he had grown old because of the wickedness in the world, and was full of his days.

11 All the generations which shall arise from this time until the day of the great judgment shall grow old quickly, before they complete two jubilees, and their knowledge shall forsake them because of their old age and all their knowledge shall vanish away.

12 In those days, if a man lives a jubilee and a-half of years, they shall say regarding him, "He has lived long," and the greater part of his days are pain and sorrow and hardship, and there is no peace. For calamity follows on calamity, and wound on wound, and hardship on hardship, and evil deeds on evil deeds, and illness on illness, and all judgments of destruction such as these, piled one on another, illness and overthrow, and snow and frost and ice, and fever, and chills, and mental and physical incapacity, and famine, and death, and sword, and captivity, and all kinds of calamities and pains.

13 All of these shall come on an evil generation, which transgresses on the earth. Their works are uncleanness and fornication, and pollution and abominations.

14 Then they shall say, "The days of the forefathers were many, lasting a thousand years, and were good; but the days of our lives, if a man lives a long life are three score years and ten, and, if he is strong, four score years, and those evil, and there is no peace in the days of this evil generation."

15 In that generation the sons shall convict their fathers and their elders of sin and unrighteousness, and of the words of their mouths and the great wickedness which they perform, and concerning their forsaking the covenant which the Lord made between them and Him. They should observe and do all His commandments and His ordinances and all His laws, without departing either to the right hand or the left.

16 For all have done evil, and every mouth speaks sinfully and all their works are unclean and an abomination, and all their ways are pollution, uncleanness, and destruction.

17 The earth shall be destroyed because of all their works, and there shall be no fruit (seed) of the vine, and no oil; for their actions are altogether faithless, and they shall all perish together, beasts and cattle and birds, and all the fish of the sea, because of the children of men.

18 They shall quarrel with one another, the young with the old, and the old with the young, the poor with the rich, the lowly with the great, and the beggar with the prince, because of the law and the covenant; for they have forgotten the commandments, and covenant, and feasts, and months, and Sabbaths, and jubilees, and all judgments.

19 They shall use swords and war to turn them back to the way, but they shall not return until much blood has been shed on the earth, one by another.

20 Those who have escaped shall not return from their wickedness to the way of righteousness, but they shall all raise themselves to a high status through deceit and wealth, that they may each steal all that belongs of his neighbor, and they shall name the great name (of God), but not in truth and not in righteousness, and they shall defile the holy of holies with their uncleanness and the corruption of their pollution.

21 A great punishment shall come because of the deeds of this generation, and the Lord will give them over to the sword and to judgment and to slavery, and to be plundered and consumed.

22 And He will arouse the Gentile sinners against them, who have neither mercy nor compassion, and who shall respect no one, neither old nor young, nor any one, for they are more wicked, strong, and evil than all the children of men.

23 They shall use violence against Israel and shall violate Jacob, and much blood shall be shed on the earth, and there shall be none to gather the dead and none to bury them.

24 In those days they shall cry aloud, and call and pray that they may be saved from the hand of the sinners, the Gentiles. But none shall be excluded (none shall be saved).

25 The heads of the children shall be white with grey hair, and a child of three weeks shall appear old like a man of one hundred years, and their work and worth shall be destroyed by hardship and oppression.

26 In those days the children shall begin to study the laws, and to seek the commandments, and to return to the path of righteousness.

27 The days shall begin to grow many and increase among those children of men until their days draw close to one thousand years, and to a greater number of years than before age was recorded.

28 There shall be neither old man nor one who is aged, for all shall be as children and youths.

29 All their days shall be full and they shall live in peace and in joy, and there shall be neither Satan nor any evil destroyer because all their days shall be days of blessing and healing.

30 And at that time the Lord will heal His servants, and they shall rise up and see great peace, and drive out their adversaries. The righteous shall understand and be thankful, and rejoice with joy forever and ever, and they shall see all their judgments and all their curses enacted on their enemies.

31 Their bones shall rest in the earth, and their spirits shall have much joy, and they shall know that it is the Lord who executes judgment, and shows mercy to hundreds and thousands and to all that love Him.

32 Moses, write down these words. Write them and record them on the heavenly tablets for a testimony for the generations forever.

[Chapter *24*]

1 It happened after the death of Abraham, that the Lord blessed Isaac his son, who arose from Hebron and went and dwelt at the Well of the Vision in the first year of the third week of this jubilee, seven years.

2 In the first year of the fourth week a famine began in the land, besides the first famine, which had been in the days of Abraham.

3 Jacob made lentil soup, and Esau came from the field hungry. He said to Jacob his brother, "Give me some of this red soup."

4 Jacob said to him, "Sell to me your birthright and I will give you bread, and also some of this lentil soup." And Esau said in his heart, "If I shall die what good is my birthright to me?"

5 He said to Jacob, "I give it to you." And Jacob said, "Swear to me, this day," and he swore to him.

6 And Jacob gave his brother Esau bread and soup, and he ate until he was satisfied, and Esau despised his birthright. For this reason was Esau's name called Edom (red), because of the red soup which Jacob gave him for his birthright.

7 And Jacob became the elder, and Esau was brought down from his dignity.

8 The famine covered the land, and Isaac departed to go down into Egypt in the second year of this week, and went to the king of the Philistines to Gerar, into the presence of Abimelech.

9 The Lord appeared to him and said to him, "Do not go down into Egypt. Dwell in the land that I shall tell you of, and sojourn in this land, and I will be with you and bless you.

10 For to you and to your offspring will I give all this land, and I will establish My oath which I swore to Abraham your father, and I will multiply your offspring as the stars of heaven, and will give to your offspring all this land.

11 And in your offspring shall all the nations of the earth be blessed, because your father obeyed My voice, and kept My ways and My commandments, and My laws, and My ordinances, and My covenant; and now do as you are told and dwell in this land."

12 And he dwelt in Gelar three weeks of years. And Abimelech commanded concerning him, and concerning all that was his, saying, "Any man that shall touch him or anything that is his shall surely die."

13 Isaac grew strong among the Philistines, and he got many possessions, oxen and sheep and camels and donkeys and a great household.

14 He sowed in the land of the Philistines and brought in a hundred-fold, and Isaac became very great, and the Philistines envied him.

15 Now all the wells that the servants of Abraham had dug during the life of Abraham, the Philistines had stopped them after the death of Abraham, and filled them with dirt.

16 Abimelech said to Isaac, "Go from us, for you are much mightier than we." Isaac departed from that place in the first year of the seventh week, and sojourned in the valleys of Gerar.

17 And they dug the wells of water again which the servants of Abraham, his father, had dug, and which the Philistines had filled after the death of Abraham his father, and he called their names as Abraham his father had named them.

18 The servants of Isaac dug a well in the valley, and found fresh, flowing water, and the shepherds of Gerar bickered with the shepherds of Isaac, saying, "The water is ours." Isaac called the name of the well "Perversity," because they had been perverse with us.

19 And they dug a second well, and they fought for that also, and he called its name "Enmity."

20 He left that place and they dug another well, and for that they did not fight, and he called the name of it "Room," and Isaac said, "Now the Lord has made room for us, and we have increased in the land."

21 And he went up from that place to the Well of the Oath in the first year of the first week in the forty-fourth jubilee.

22 The Lord appeared to him in the night of the new moon of the first month, and said to him, "I am the God of Abraham your father; fear not, for I am with you, and shall bless you and shall surely multiply your offspring as the sand of the earth, for the sake of Abraham my servant."

23 And he built an altar there, which Abraham his father had first built, and he called on the name of the Lord, and he offered sacrifice to the God of Abraham his father.

24 They dug a well and they found fresh, flowing water.

25 The servants of Isaac dug another well and did not find water, and they went and told Isaac that they had not found water, and Isaac said, "I have sworn this day to the Philistines and this thing has been announced to us."

26 And he called the name of that place the Well of the Oath, because there he had sworn to Abimelech and Ahuzzath, his friend, and also to Phicol, who was the commander and his host.

27 Isaac knew that day that he had sworn to them under pressure to make peace with them.

28 On that day Isaac cursed the Philistines and said, "Cursed be the Philistines to the day of wrath and indignation from among all nations. May God make them a disdain and a curse and an object of anger and indignation in the hands of the Gentile sinners and in the hands of the Kittim.

29 Whoever escapes the sword of the enemy and the Kittim, may the righteous nation root them out in judgment from under heaven. They shall be the enemies and foes of my children throughout their generations on the earth.

30 No part of them will remain. Not even one shall be spared on the day of the wrath of judgment. The offspring of the Philistines will experience destruction, rooting out, and expulsion from the earth and this is all that is in store for them. There shall not be a name or an offspring left on the earth for these Caphtorim (the seat of the Philistine state).

31 For though he rises up to heaven, he shall be brought down, and though he makes himself strong on earth, from there shall he be dragged out, and though he hide himself among the nations, even from that place shall he be rooted out.

32 Though he descends into the abode of the dead, his condemnation shall be great, and he shall have no peace there.

33 If he goes into captivity by the hands of those that seek his life they shall kill him on the way (to his imprisonment), and neither his name nor offspring shall be left on all the earth. Into an eternal curse shall he depart."

34 It is written and engraved concerning him on the heavenly tablets, that on the day of judgment he will be rooted out of the earth.

[Chapter 25]

1 In the second year of this week in this jubilee, Rebecca called Jacob her son, and spoke to him, saying, "My son, do not take a wife from the daughters of Canaan as Esau, your brother, who took two wives of the daughters of Canaan, and they have made my soul bitter with all their unclean acts, for all their actions are fornication and lust, and there is no righteousness in them, because their deeds are evil.

2 I love you greatly, my son, and my heart and my affection bless you every hour of the day and in every night.

3 Now, my son, listen to my voice, and do the will of your mother, and do not take a wife of the daughters of this land, but only from the house of my father, and of those related to my father.

4 If you will take you a wife of the house of my father, the Most High God will bless you, and your children shall be a righteous generation and a holy offspring." And then spoke Jacob to Rebecca, his mother, and said to her, "Look, mother, I am nine weeks of years old, and I have neither been with nor have I touched any woman, nor have I engaged myself to any, nor I have even thought of taking me wife of the daughters of Canaan.

5 For I remember, mother, the words of Abraham, our father, for he commanded me not to take a wife of the daughters of Canaan, but to take me a wife from the offspring of my father's house and from my kind folks.

6 I have heard before that daughters have been born to Laban, your brother, and I have set my heart on them to take a wife from among them.

7 For this reason I have guarded myself in my spirit against sinning or being corrupted in any way throughout all the days of my life; for with regard to lust and fornication, Abraham, my father, gave me many commands.

8 Despite all that he has commanded me, these two and twenty years my brother has argued with me, and spoken frequently to me and said, "My brother, take a wife that is a sister of my two wives," but I refused to do as he has done.

9 I swear before you mother, that all the days of my life I will not take me a wife from the daughters of the offspring of Canaan, and I will not act wickedly as my brother has done.

10 Do not be afraid mother, be assured that I shall do your will and walk in uprightness, and not corrupt my ways forever."

11 When she heard this, she lifted up her face to heaven and extended the fingers of her hands, and opened her mouth and blessed the Most High God, who had created the heaven and the earth, and she gave Him thanks and praise.

12 She said, "Blessed be the Lord God, and may His holy name be blessed forever and ever. He has given me Jacob as a pure son and a holy offspring; for he is Yours, and Yours shall his offspring be continually, throughout all the generations forever.

13 Bless him, O Lord, and place in my mouth the blessing of righteousness, that I may bless him."

14 At that hour, when the spirit of righteousness descended into her mouth, she placed both her hands on the head of Jacob, and said, "Blessed are You, Lord of righteousness and God of the ages, and may You bless him beyond all the generations of men.

15 My Son, may He give you the path of righteousness, and reveal righteousness to your offspring.

16 May He make your sons many during your life, and may they arise according to the number of the months of the year. And may their sons become many and great beyond the stars of heaven, and may their numbers be more than the sand of the sea.

17 May He give them this good and pleasing land, as He said He would give it to Abraham and to his offspring after him always, and may they hold it as a possession forever.

18 My son, may I see blessed children born to you during my life, and may all your offspring be blessed and holy.

19 And as you have refreshed your mother's spirit during her life, the womb of her that gave birth to you blesses you now. My affection and my heart (breasts) bless you and my mouth and my tongue greatly praise you.

20 Increase and spread over the earth. May your offspring be perfect in the joy of heaven and earth forever. May your offspring rejoice, and on the great day of peace may they have peace.

21 May your name and your offspring endure to all the ages, and may the Most High God be their God, and may the God of righteousness dwell with them, and may His sanctuary be built by you all the ages.

22 Blessed be he that blesses you, and all flesh that curses you falsely, may it be cursed."

23 And she kissed him, and said to him, "May the Lord of the world love you as the heart of your mother and her affection rejoice in you and bless you." And she ceased from blessing.

[Chapter *26*]

1 In the seventh year of this week Isaac called Esau, his elder son, and said to him, " I am old, my son, and my sight is dim, and I do not know the day of my death.

2 Now, take your hunting weapons, your quiver, and your bow, and go out to the field, and hunt and catch me venison, my son, and make me flavorful meat, like my soul loves, and bring it to me that I may eat, and that my soul may bless you before I die."

3 But Rebecca heard Isaac speaking to Esau.

4 Esau went out early to the field to hunt and catch and bring home meat to his father.

5 Rebecca called Jacob, her son, and said to him, "Look, I heard Isaac, your father, speak to Esau, your brother, saying, "Hunt for me, and make me flavorful meat, and bring it to me that I may eat and bless you before the Lord before I die."

6 Now, my son, do as you are told and do as I command you. Go to your flock and fetch me two good kids of the goats, and I will make them good tasting meat for your father, like he loves, and you will bring it to your father that he may eat and bless you to the Lord before he dies."

7 Jacob said to Rebecca his mother, "Mother, I shall not withhold anything which my father would eat and which would please him, but I am afraid that he will recognize my voice and wish to touch me.

8 And you know that I am smooth, and Esau, my brother, is hairy, and I he will see me an evildoer because I am doing something that he has not told me to do and he will be very angry with me, and I shall bring on myself a curse, and not a blessing."

9 Rebecca, his mother, said to him, "Your curse be on me, my son, just do as you are told."

10 Jacob obeyed the voice of Rebecca, his mother, and went and brought back two good and fat goat kids, and brought them to his mother, and his mother made them tasty meat like he loved.

11 Rebecca took the good and pleasing clothes of Esau, her elder son, which was with her in the house, and she clothed Jacob, her younger son, with them, and she put the skins of the kids on his hands and on the exposed parts of his neck.

12 And she gave the meat and the bread, which she had prepared, to her son Jacob.

13 Jacob went in to his father and said, "I am your son. I have done as you asked me. Arise and sit and eat of that which I have caught, father, that your soul may bless me."

14 Isaac said to his son, "How have you found game so quickly, my son?"

15 Jacob said, "Because the Lord your God caused me to find."

16 Isaac said to him, "Come closer, that I may feel you, my son, and know if you are my son Esau or not."

17 Jacob went near to Isaac, his father, and he felt him and said, "The voice is Jacob's voice, but the hands are the hands of Esau," and he did not recognize him, because it was a decision from heaven to remove his power of perception and Isaac discerned not, because his hands were hairy as his brother Esau's, so Isaac blessed him.

18 He said, "Are you my son Esau? " and Jacob said, "I am your son," and Isaac said, "Bring it to me that I may eat of that which you have caught, my son, that my soul may bless you."

19 And Jacob brought it to him, and he ate, and Jacob brought him wine and he drank.

20 Isaac, his father, said to him, "Come close and kiss me, my son."

21 He came close and kissed Isaac. And he smelled the smell of his raiment, and he blessed Jacob and said, "Look, the smell of my son is as the smell of a full field which the Lord has blessed.

22 May the Lord give you of the dew of heaven and of the dew of the earth, and plenty of corn and oil. Let nations serve you and peoples bow down to you.

23 Be ruler over your brothers, and let your mother's sons bow down to you; and may all the blessings that the Lord has blessed me and blessed Abraham, my father, be imparted to you and to your offspring forever. Cursed be he that curses you, and blessed be he that blesses you."

The Book of Jubilees

24 It happened as soon as Isaac had made an end of blessing his son Jacob, that Jacob had went away from Isaac his father and hid himself.

25 Esau, his brother, came in from his hunting. And he also made flavorful meat, and brought it to his father and Esau said to his father, "Let my father arise, and eat of my venison that your soul may bless me."

26 Isaac, his father, said to him, "Who are you?" Esau said to him, "I am your first born, your son Esau. I have done as you have commanded me."

27 Isaac was very greatly surprised, and said, "Who is he that has hunted and caught and brought it to me, and I have eaten of all before you came, and have blessed him, and he shall be blessed, and all his offspring forever."

28 It happened when Esau heard the words of his father Isaac that he cried with a very loud and bitter cry, and said to his father, "Bless me also, father!"

29 Isaac said to him, "Your brother came with trickery, and has taken away your blessing."

30 He said, "Now I know why his name is Jacob. Behold, he has supplanted me these two times, he took away my birthright, and now he has taken away my blessing."

31 Esau said, "Have you not reserved a blessing for me, father?" and Isaac answered and said to Esau, "Look, I have made him your lord, and all his brothers have I given to him for servants. I have strengthened him with plenty of corn and wine and oil. Now what shall I do for you, my son?"

32 Esau said to Isaac, his father, "Have you only one blessing, father? Please. Bless me, also, father."

33 Esau lifted up his voice and wept. And Isaac answered and said to him, "Far from the dew of the earth shall be your dwelling, and far from the dew of heaven from above.

34 By your sword will you live, and you will serve your brother.

35 It shall happen that when you become great, and do shake his yoke from off your neck, you will sin completely and commit a sin worthy of death, and your offspring shall be rooted out from under heaven."

36 Esau kept threatening Jacob because of the blessing his father blessed him with, and he said in his heart, "May the days of mourning for my father come now, so that I may kill my brother Jacob."

[Chapter 27]

1 Rebecca was told Esau's words in a dream, and Rebecca sent for Jacob her younger son, and said to him, "Look, Esau, your brother, will take vengeance on you and kill you.

2 Now, therefore, my son, do as you are told, and get up and flee to Laban, my brother, to Haran, and stay with him a few days until your brother's anger fades away, and he removes his anger from you, and forgets all that you have done. Then I will send for you to come from that place."

3 Jacob said, "I am not afraid. If he wishes to kill me, I will kill him."

4 But she said to him, "Let me not be bereft of both my sons on one day."

5 Jacob said to Rebecca, his mother, "Look, you know that my father has become old, and does not see because his eyes are dull. If I leave him he will think it is wrong. If I leave him and go away from you, my father will be angry and will curse me.

6 I will not go. When he sends me, only then will I go."

7 Rebecca said to Jacob, "I will go in and speak to him, and he will send you away."

8 Rebecca went in and said to Isaac, "I hate my life because of the two daughters of Heth, whom Esau has taken as wives. If Jacob take a wife from among the daughters of the land such as these, I could not live with it, because the daughters of Canaan are evil."

9 Isaac called Jacob and blessed him, and warned him and said to him, "Do not take you a wife of any of the daughters of Canaan. Arise and go to Mesopotamia, to the house of Bethuel, your mother's father, and take a wife from that place of the daughters of Laban, your mother's brother.

10 And God Almighty bless you and increase and multiply you that you may become a company of nations, and give you the blessings of my father, Abraham, to you and to your offspring after you, that you may inherit the land that you travel in and all the land which God gave to Abraham. Go in peace, my son."

11 Isaac sent Jacob away, and he went to Mesopotamia, to Laban the son of Bethuel the Syrian, the brother of Rebecca, Jacob's mother.

12 It happened after Jacob had departed to Mesopotamia that the spirit of Rebecca was grieved for her son, and she wept.

13 Isaac said to Rebecca, "My sister, weep not because of Jacob, my son, for he goes in peace, and in peace will he return.

14 The Most High God will preserve him from all evil and will be with him. He will not forsake him all his days, for I know that his ways will be made to prosper in all things wherever he goes, until he return in peace to us, and we see him in peace. Fear not on his account, my sister, for he is on the upright path and he is a perfect man, and he is faithful and will not perish. Weep not."

15 Isaac comforted Rebecca because of her son Jacob, and blessed him.

16 Jacob went from the Well of the Oath to go to Haran on the first year of the second week in the forty-fourth jubilee, and he came to Luz on the mountains, that is, Bethel, on the new moon of the first month of this week, and he came to the place at dusk and turned from the way to the west of the road that is close, and that night he slept there, for the sun had set.

17 He took one of the stones of that place (as a pillow) and laid down under the tree, and he was journeying alone, and he slept.

18 Jacob dreamt that night, and saw a ladder set up on the earth, and the top of it reached to heaven, and he saw the angels of the Lord ascended and descended on it, and behold, the Lord stood on it.

19 And He spoke to Jacob and said, "I am the Lord God of Abraham, your father, and the God of Isaac. The land you are sleeping on I will give to you and to your offspring after you.

20 Your offspring shall be as the dust of the earth, and you will increase to the west and to the east, to the north and the south, and in you and in your offspring shall all the families of the nations be blessed.

21 Behold, I will be with you, and will keep you wherever you go. I will bring you into this land again in peace. I will not leave you until I do everything that I told you."

22 Jacob awoke from his sleep and said, "Truly this place is the house of the Lord, and I did not know it."

23 He was afraid and said, "I am afraid because this place is none other than the house of God, and this is the gate of heaven, and I did not know it."

24 Jacob got up early in the morning, and took the stone that he had placed under his head and set it up as a pillar for a sign. And he poured oil on the top of it. And he called the name of that place Bethel, but the name of the place was previously Luz.

25 And Jacob vowed a vow to the Lord, saying, "If the Lord will be with me, and will keep me in the way that I go, and give me bread to eat and clothes to put on, so that I come again to my father's house in peace, then the Lord shall be my God, and this stone which I have set up as a pillar for a sign in this place shall be the Lord's house, and of all that you gave me, I shall give the tenth to you, my God."

[Chapter 28]

1 He went on his journey, and came to the land of the east, to Laban, the brother of Rebecca, and he was with him, and Jacob served Laban for Rachel his daughter one week of years. In the first year of the third week of years he said to him, "Give me my wife, for whom I have served you seven years ," and Laban said to Jacob, "I will give you your wife."

2 Laban made a feast, and took Leah his elder daughter, and gave her to Jacob as a wife, and gave Leah Zilpah for a handmaid; and Jacob did not know, for he thought that she was Rachel.

3 He went in to her, and saw she was Leah; and Jacob was angry with Laban, and said to him, "Why have you done this to me?

4 Did I not serve you for Rachel and not for Leah? Why have you wronged me?

5 Take your daughter, and I will go. You have done evil to me." For Jacob loved Rachel more than Leah because Leah's eyes were weak, but her form was very beautiful. Rachel had beautiful eyes and a beautiful and very voluptuous form.

6 Laban said to Jacob, "It is not done that way in our country, we do not to give the younger before the elder." And it is not right to do this; for thus it is ordained and written in the heavenly tablets, that no one should give his younger daughter before the elder; but the elder one is given first and after her the younger. The man who does so will have guilt placed against him in heaven, and none is righteous that does this thing, for this deed is evil before the Lord.

7 Command the children of Israel that they not do this thing. Let them neither take nor give the younger before they have given the elder, for it is very wicked."

8 And Laban said to Jacob, "Let the seven days of the feast pass by, and I shall give you Rachel, that you may serve me another seven years, that you may pasture my sheep as you did in the former week (of years)."

9 On the day when the seven days of the feast of Leah had passed, Laban gave Rachel to Jacob, that he might serve him another seven years, and he gave Rachel, Bilhah, the sister of Zilpah, as a handmaid.

10 He served yet other seven years for Rachel, for Leah had been given to him for nothing, since it was Rachel he wanted.

11 And the Lord opened the womb of Leah, and she conceived and gave birth to a son for Jacob, and he called his name Reuben, on the fourteenth day of the ninth month, in the first year of the third week.

12 But the womb of Rachel was closed, for the Lord saw that Leah was hated and Rachel loved.

13 Again Jacob went in to Leah, and she conceived, and gave birth to a second son for Jacob, and he called his name Simeon, on the twenty-first of the tenth month, and in the third year of this week.

14 Again Jacob went in to Leah, and she conceived, and gave birth to a third son, and he called his name Levi, in the new moon of the first month in the sixth year of this week.

15 Again Jacob went in to her, and she conceived, and gave birth to a fourth son, and he called his name Judah, on the fifteenth of the third month, in the first year of the fourth week.

16 Because of all this Rachel envied Leah, for she did not bear a child, and she said to Jacob, "Give me children;" and Jacob said, "Have I withheld from you the fruits of your womb? Have I left you?"

17 And when Rachel saw that Leah had given birth to four sons for Jacob: Reuben and Simeon and Levi and Judah, she said to him, "Go in to Bilhah my handmaid, and she will conceive, and bear a son for me."

18 She gave him Bilhah, her handmaid, to wife. And he went in to her, and she conceived, and gave birth to a son, and he called his name Dan, on the ninth of the sixth month, in the sixth year of the third week.

19 Jacob went in again to Bilhah a second time, and she conceived, and gave birth to another son for Jacob, and Rachel called his name Napthali, on the fifth of the seventh month, in the second year of the fourth week.

20 When Leah saw that she had become sterile and could no longer have children, she envied Rachel, and she also gave her handmaid Zilpah to Jacob to wife, and she conceived, and gave birth to a son, and Leah called his name Gad, on the twelfth of the eighth month, in the third year of the fourth week.

21 He went in to her again, and she conceived and gave birth to a second son, and Leah called his name Asher, on the second of the eleventh month, in the fifth year of the fourth week.

22 Jacob went in to Leah, and she conceived, and gave birth to a son, and she called his name Issachar, on the fourth of the fifth month, in the fourth year of the fourth week, and she gave him to a nurse.

23 Jacob went in again to her, and she conceived, and gave birth to two children, a son and a daughter, and she called the name of the son Zabulon, and the name of the daughter Dinah, in the seventh day of the seventh month, in the sixth year of the fourth week.

24 The Lord was gracious to Rachel, and opened her womb, and she conceived, and gave birth to a son, and she called his name Joseph, on the new moon of the fourth month, in the sixth year in this fourth week.

25 In the days when Joseph was born, Jacob said to Laban, "Give me my wives and sons, and let me go to my father Isaac, and let me make a household for myself; for I have completed the years in which I have served you for your two daughters, and I will go to the house of my father."

26 Laban said to Jacob, "Stay with me and I will pay you wages, and pasture my flock for me again, and take your wages."

27 They agreed with one another that he should give him as his wages those of the lambs and kids which were born spotted black and white, these were to be his wages.

28 All the sheep brought out spotted and speckled and black, variously marked, and they brought out again lambs like themselves, and all that were spotted were Jacob's and those which were not spotted were Laban's.

29 Jacob's possessions multiplied greatly, and he possessed oxen and sheep and donkeys and camels, and men-servants and maid-servants.

30 Laban and his sons envied Jacob, and Laban took back his sheep from him, and he envied him and watched him for an opportunity to do evil.

[Chapter *29*]

1 It happened when Rachel had given birth to Joseph, that Laban went to shear his sheep; for they were distant from him, a three-day journey.

2 Jacob saw that Laban was going to shear his sheep, and Jacob called Leah and Rachel, and spoke sweetly to them in order to convince them to come with him to the land of Canaan.

3 For he told them how he had seen everything in a dream. All that God had spoken to him that he should return to his father's house, and they said, "To every place where you go we will go with you."

4 Jacob blessed the God of Isaac his father, and the God of Abraham his father's father, and he arose and placed his wives and his children on donkeys, and took all his possessions and crossed the river, and came to the land of Gilead, and Jacob hid his intention from Laban and did not tell him.

5 In the seventh year of the fourth week Jacob turned his face toward Gilead in the first month, on the twenty-first of it.

6 Laban pursued and overtook Jacob in the mountain of Gilead in the third month, on the thirteenth of it. And the Lord did not permit him to injure Jacob for he appeared to him in a dream by night.

7 Laban spoke to Jacob. On the fifteenth of those days Jacob made a feast for Laban, and for all who came with him, and Jacob swore to Laban that day, and Laban also swore to Jacob, that neither should cross the mountain of Gilead to do evil to the other.

8 He made a heap (of stones) for a witness there; wherefore the name of that place is called, "The Heap of Witness," after this heap.

9 But before they used to call the land of Gilead the land of the Rephaim. The Rephaim were born giants whose height was ten, nine, eight, down to seven cubits.

10 Their dwelling place was from the land of the children of Ammon to Mount Hermon, and the seats of their kingdom were Karnaim and Ashtaroth, and Edrei, and Misur, and Beon.

11 The Lord destroyed them because of the evil of their deeds, for they were malevolent, and the Amorites were wicked and sinful. There is no people today which has committed the full range of their sins, and their life on the earth was shortened.

12 Jacob sent Laban away, and he departed into Mesopotamia, the land of the East, and Jacob returned to the land of Gilead.

13 He passed over the Jabbok in the ninth month, on the eleventh of it. On that day Esau, his brother, came to him, and he was reconciled to him, and departed from him to the land of Seir, but Jacob dwelt in tents.

14 In the first year of the fifth week in this jubilee he crossed the Jordan, and dwelt beyond the Jordan. He pastured his sheep from the sea of the heap to Bethshan, and to Dothan and to the forest of Akrabbim.

15 He sent his father Isaac all of his possessions such as clothing, and food, and meat, and drink, and milk, and butter, and cheese, and some dates of the valley.

16 Four times a year, he sent gifts to his mother Rebecca who was living at the tower of Abraham. He sent the gifts between the times of the months between plowing and reaping, and between autumn and the rain season, and between winter and spring.

17 For Isaac had returned from the Well of the Oath and gone up to the tower of his father Abraham, and he dwelt there apart from his son Esau.

18 For in the days when Jacob went to Mesopotamia, Esau took to himself a wife Mahalath, the daughter of Ishmael, and he gathered together all the flocks of his father and his wives, and went up and dwelt on Mount Seir, and left Isaac his father at the Well of the Oath alone.

19 And Isaac went up from the Well of the Oath and dwelt in the tower of Abraham his father on the mountains of Hebron, and that is where Jacob sent all that he did send to his father and his mother from time to time, all they needed, and they blessed Jacob with all their heart and with all their soul.

[Chapter *30*]

1 In the first year of the sixth week he went up to Salem, to the east of Shechem, in the fourth month, and he went in peace. Shechem, the son of Hamor, the Hivite, the prince of the land carried off Dinah, the daughter of Jacob, into the house, and he had sex with her and defiled her. She was a little girl, a child of twelve years.

2 He begged his father and her brothers that she might be given to him as a wife.

3 Jacob and his sons were very angry because of the men of Shechem, for they had defiled Dinah, their sister. They spoke to them while planning evil acts and they dealt deceitfully with them and tricked them.

4 Simeon and Levi came unexpectedly to Shechem and executed judgment on all the men of Shechem, and killed all the men whom they found in it. They did not leave a single one remaining in it. They killed all in hand to hand battle because they had dishonored their sister Dinah.

5 Let it not again be done from now on that a daughter of Israel be defiled. Judgment is ordained in heaven against them that they should destroy all the men of the Shechemites with the sword because they had committed shame in Israel.

6 The Lord delivered them into the hands of the sons of Jacob that they might exterminate them with the sword and execute judgment on them. That it might not again be done in Israel that a virgin of Israel should be defiled.

7 If there is any man in Israel who wishes to give his daughter or his sister to any man who is of the offspring of the Gentiles he shall surely die. They shall stone him, for he has committed shame in Israel. They shall burn the woman with fire, because she has dishonored the name of the house of her father, and she shall be rooted out of Israel.

8 Do not let an adulteress and let no uncleanness be found in Israel throughout all the days of the generations of the earth. For Israel is holy to the Lord, and every man who has defiled it shall surely die. They shall stone him.

9 For it has been ordained and written in the heavenly tablets regarding all the offspring of Israel. He who defiles it shall surely die. He shall be killed by stoning. There is no limit of days for this law. There is no remission, and no atonement.

10 The man who has defiled his daughter shall be rooted out from every corner of all Israel, because he has given of his offspring to Moloch (a pagan God, the worship of which involved burning the child alive), and committed impurity and defiled his child.

11 Moses, command the children of Israel and exhort them not to give their daughters to the Gentiles, and not to take for their sons any of the daughters of the Gentiles, for this is abominable before the Lord.

12 It is because of this that I have written all the deeds of the Shechemites, which they committed against Dinah, and placed them in the words of the Law for you. I have also written how the sons of Jacob spoke, saying, "We will not give our daughter to a man who is uncircumcised, for that is a reproach to us."

13 It is a reproach to Israel that anyone take the daughters of the Gentiles, for this is unclean and abominable to Israel.

14 Israel will not be free from this uncleanness if it has a wife of the daughters of the Gentiles, or has given any of its daughters to a man who is of any of the Gentiles.

15 There will be plague upon plague, and curse upon curse, and every judgment and plague and curse will come if he does this thing, or if they ignore those who commit uncleanness, or defile the sanctuary of the Lord, or those who profane His holy name. If any of these happen the whole nation together will be judged for all the uncleanness and profanation of this man.

16 There will be no judging people by their position and no receiving fruits, or offerings, or burnt-offerings, or fat, or the fragrance of sweet odor from his hands. It will be unacceptable and so warn every man and woman in Israel who defiles the sanctuary.

17 For this reason I have commanded you, saying, "Give this testimony to Israel, see how the Shechemites and their sons fared? See how they were delivered into the hands of two sons of Jacob, and they killed them under torture? It was counted to them for righteousness, and it is written down to them for righteousness.

18 The offspring of Levi were chosen for the priesthood, and to be Levites, that they might minister before the Lord, as we do, continually. Levi and his sons will be blessed forever, for he was zealous to execute righteousness and judgment and vengeance on all those who arose against Israel.

19 So they wrote a testimony in his favor of blessing and righteousness on the heavenly tablets in the presence of the God of all.

20 We remember the righteousness that the man fulfilled during his life, throughout the years, until a thousand generations they will record it. It will come to him and to his descendants after him, and he has been recorded on the heavenly tablets as a friend and a righteous man.

21 All this account I have written for you, and have commanded you to tell the children of Israel, so that they will not commit sin nor transgress the laws nor break the covenant which has been ordained for them. They should fulfill it and be recorded as friends (of God).

22 But if they transgress and work uncleanness in any way, they will be recorded on the heavenly tablets as adversaries (of God), and they will be blotted out of the book of life. Instead, they will be recorded in the book of those who will be destroyed and with those who will be rooted out of the earth.

23 On the day when the sons of Jacob killed Shechem it was written in the record in their favor in heaven that they had executed righteousness and uprightness and vengeance on the sinners, and it was written for a blessing.

24 They brought Dinah, their sister, out of the house of Shechem. They took everything that was in Shechem captive. They took their sheep and their oxen and their donkeys, and all their wealth, and all their flocks, and brought them all to Jacob their father.

25 He reproached them because they had put the city to the sword for he feared those who dwelt in the land, the Canaanites and the Perizzites.

26 The dread of the Lord was on all the cities that are near Shechem. They did not fight or chase after the sons of Jacob, for terror had fallen on them.

[Chapter *31*]

1 On the new moon of the month, Jacob spoke to all the people of his house, saying, "Purify yourselves and change your clothes, and let us get up and go to Bethel where I vowed a vow to Him on the day when I fled from Esau my brother. Let us do this because God has been with me and brought me into this land in peace. You must put away the strange gods that you raise among you."

2 They gave up the strange gods and that which was in their ears and which was on their necks and the idols which Rachel stole from Laban her father she gave wholly to Jacob. And he burnt and broke them to pieces and destroyed them, and hid them under an oak, which is in the land of Shechem.

3 He went up on the new moon of the seventh month to Bethel. And he built an altar at the place where he had slept, and he set up a pillar there, and he sent word to his father,

Isaac, and his mother, Rebecca. He asked to come to Isaac. There, Jacob wished to offer his sacrifice.

4 Isaac said, "Let my son, Jacob, come, and let me see him before I die."

5 Jacob went to his father, Isaac, and his mother, Rebecca, to the house of his father Abraham, and he took two of his sons with him, Levi and Judah.

6 Rebecca came out from the tower to the front of it to kiss Jacob and embrace him, for her spirit had revived when she heard, "Look Jacob your son has come," and she kissed him.

7 She saw his two sons and she recognized them. She said to him, "Are these your sons, my son?" and she embraced them and kissed them, and blessed them, saying, "In you shall the offspring of Abraham become illustrious, and you shall prove a blessing on the earth."

8 Jacob went in to Isaac his father, to the room where he lay, and his two sons were with him. He took his father's hand, stooped down, he kissed him. Isaac held on to the neck of Jacob his son, and wept on his neck.

9 The darkness left the eyes of Isaac, and he saw the two sons of Jacob, Levi, and Judah. And he said, "Are these your sons, my son? Because they look like you."

10 He said to Isaac, "They were truly my sons, and you have clearly seen that they are truly my sons."

11 They came near to him, and he turned and kissed them and embraced them both together.

12 The spirit of prophecy came down into his mouth, and he took Levi by his right hand and Judah by his left.

13 He turned to Levi first, and began to bless him first, and said to him, "May the God of all, the very Lord of all the ages, bless you and your children throughout all the ages.

14 May the Lord give to you and your offspring greatness and great glory from among all flesh. May the Lord cause you and your offspring to draw near to Him to serve in His sanctuary like the angels of the presence (of the Lord) and as the holy ones. The offspring of your sons shall be for the glory and greatness and holiness of God. May He make them great throughout all the ages. They shall be judges and princes, and chiefs of all the offspring of the sons of Jacob. They shall speak the word of the Lord in righteousness, and they shall judge all His judgments in righteousness.

15 They shall declare My ways to Jacob and My paths to Israel. The blessing of the Lord shall be given in their mouths to bless all the offspring of the beloved.

16 Your mother has called your name Levi, and rightly has she called your name. You will be joined to the Lord and be the companion of all the sons of Jacob. Let His table be your table, and let your sons eat from it. May your table be full throughout all generations, and let your food not fail in all the ages.

17 Let all who hate you fall down before you, and let all your adversaries be rooted out and perish. Blessed be he that blesses you, and cursed be every nation that curses you."

18 To Judah he said, "May the Lord give you strength and power to put all that hate you under your feet. You and one of your sons will be a prince over the sons of Jacob. May your name and the name of your sons go out across every land and region.

19 Then shall the Gentiles fear you, and all the nations and people shall shake (with fear of you). In you will be the help of Jacob, and in you will be found the salvation of Israel.

20 When you sit on the throne, which honors of your righteousness, there shall be great peace for all the offspring of the sons of the beloved. Blessed be he that blesses you, and cursed be all that hate you, afflict you, or curse you. They shall be rooted out and destroyed from the earth."

21 He turned, kissed him again, and embraced him, and rejoiced greatly because he had seen the sons of his son, Jacob, clearly and truly.

22 He stepped out from between his feet and fell down. He bowed down to him, and blessed them. He rested there with Isaac, his father, that night, and they ate and drank with joy.

23 He made the two sons of Jacob sleep, the one on his right hand and the other on his left. It was counted to him for righteousness.

24 Jacob told his father everything during the night about how the Lord had shown him great mercy, and how he had caused him to prosper in all his ways, and how he protected him from all evil.

25 Isaac blessed the God of his father Abraham, who had not withdrawn his mercy and his righteousness from the sons of his servant Isaac.

26 In the morning, Jacob told his father, Isaac, the vow, which he had vowed to the Lord. He told him of the vision which he had seen, and that he had built an altar. He told him that everything was ready for the sacrifice to be made before the Lord as he had vowed. He had come to set him on a donkey.

27 Isaac said to Jacob his son, "I am not able to go with you, for I am old and not able to endure the way. Go in peace, my son. I am one hundred and sixty-five years this day. I am no longer able to journey. Set your mother on a donkey and let her go with you.

28 I know that you have come on my account, my son. May this day be blessed on which you have seen me alive, and I also have seen you, my son.

29 May you prosper and fulfill the vow that you have vowed. Do not put off your vow, for you will be called to account for the vow. Now hurry to perform it, and may He who has made all things be pleased. It is to Him you have vowed the vow."

30 He said to Rebecca, "Go with Jacob your son," and Rebecca went with Jacob her son, and Deborah with her, and they came to Bethel.

31 Jacob remembered the prayer with which his father had blessed him and his two sons, Levi and Judah. He rejoiced and blessed the God of his fathers, Abraham and Isaac.

32 He said, "Now I know that my sons and I have an eternal hope in the God of all." Thus is it ordained concerning the two. They recorded it as an eternal testimony to them on the heavenly tablets how Isaac blessed his sons.

[Chapter *32*]

1 That night he stayed at Bethel, and Levi dreamed that they had ordained and made his sons and him the priests of the Most High God forever. Then he awoke from his sleep and blessed the Lord.

2 Jacob rose early in the morning, on the fourteenth of this month, and he gave a tithe for all that came with him, both of men and cattle, both of gold and every vessel and garment. Yes, he gave tithes of all.

3 In those days Rachel became pregnant with her son Benjamin. Jacob counted his sons starting from him and going to the oldest and Levi fell to the portion of the Lord. (Levi was the third son – three is the number of spiritual completeness.) His father clothed him in the garments of the priesthood and filled his hands.

4 On the fifteenth of this month, he brought fourteen oxen from among the cattle, and twenty-eight rams, and forty-nine sheep, and seven lambs, and twenty-one kids of the goats to the altar as a burnt-offering on the altar of sacrifice. The offering was well pleasing and a sweet odor before God.

5 This was his offering, done in acknowledgement of the vow in which he had promised that he would give a tenth, with their fruit-offerings and their drink- offerings.

6 When the fire had consumed it, he burnt incense over the fire, and for a thank-offering he sacrificed two oxen and four rams and four sheep, four male goats, and two sheep of a year old, and two kids of the goats. This he did daily for seven days.

7 He, his men, and all his sons were eating this with joy during seven days and blessing and thanking the Lord, who had delivered him out of all his tribulation and had given him His promise.

8 He tithed all the clean animals, and made a burnt sacrifice, but he did not give the unclean animals to Levi his son. He gave him (responsibility for) all the souls of the men. Levi acted in the priestly office at Bethel in the presence of Jacob his father, in preference to his ten brothers. He was a priest there, and Jacob gave his vow, and he gave a tithe to the Lord again and sanctified it, and it became holy to Him.

9 For this reason it is ordained on the heavenly tablets as a law for the offering of the tithe should be eaten in the presence of the Lord every year, in the place where it is chosen that His name should live and reside. This law has no limit of days forever.

10 This law is written so that it may be fulfilled every year. The second tithe should be eaten in the presence of the Lord, in the place where it has been chosen, and nothing shall be left over from it from this year to the following year.

11 In its year shall the seed be eaten until the days of the gathering of the seed of the year. The wine shall be consumed until the days of the wine, and the oil until the days of its season.

12 All that is left of it and all that becomes old will be regarded as spoiled, let it be burnt with fire, for it is unclean.

13 Let them eat it together in the sanctuary, and let them not permit it to become old.

14 All the tithes of the oxen and sheep shall be holy to the Lord, and shall belong to His priests. They will eat before Him from year to year, for thus is it ordained and written on the heavenly tablets regarding the tithe.

15 On the following night, on the twenty-second day of this month, Jacob resolved to build that place and to surround the court with a wall, and to sanctify it and make it holy forever, for himself and his children after him.

16 The Lord appeared to him by night and blessed him and said to him, "Your name shall not be called Jacob, but they will call your name Israel."

17 And He said to him again, "I am the Lord who created the heaven and the earth, and I will increase you and multiply you greatly, and kings shall come forth from you, and they shall be judges everywhere the foot of the sons of men have walked.

18 I will give to your offspring all the earth that is under heaven. They shall judge all the nations, as they desire. After that they shall possess the entire earth and inherit it forever."

19 And He finished speaking with him, and He went up from him.

20 Jacob watched until He had ascended into heaven.

21 In a vision at night he saw an angel descend from heaven with seven tablets in his hands, and he gave them to Jacob, and he read them and knew all that was written on it that would happen to him and his sons throughout all the ages.

22 He showed him all that was written on the tablets, and said to him, "Do not build on this place, and do not make it an eternal sanctuary, and do not live here. This is not the place. Go to the house of Abraham your father and live with Isaac, your father, until the day he dies.

23 For in Egypt you will die in peace, and in this land you will be buried with honor in the sepulcher of your fathers, with Abraham and Isaac.

24 Do not fear. As you have seen and read it shall all be. Write down everything that you have seen and read."

25 Jacob said, "Lord, how can I remember all that I have read and seen?" He said to him, "I will bring all things to your remembrance."

26 He ascended from Jacob, and Jacob awoke from his sleep. He remembered everything that he had read and seen, and he wrote down all the words.

27 He celebrated there yet another day, and he sacrificed on that day as he had sacrificed on all the former days. He called its name "Addition," because this day was added, and the former days he called "The Feast."

28 It was made known and revealed to him and it is written on the heavenly tablets that he should celebrate the day, and add it to the seven days of the feast.

29 Its name was called "Addition," because that it was recorded among the days of the feast days, according to the number of the days of the year.

30 In the night, on the twenty-third of this month, Deborah, Rebecca's nurse died, and they buried her beneath the city under the oak of the river. He called the name of this place, "The river of Deborah," and he called the oak, "The oak of the mourning of Deborah."

31 Rebecca departed and returned to her house, to his father Isaac. Jacob sent rams and sheep and male goats by her so that she should prepare a meal for his father such as he desired.

32 He followed his mother until he came to the land of Kabratan, and he lived there.

33 Rachel gave birth to a son in the night, and called his name "son of my sorrow", for she broke down while giving birth to him, but his father called his name Benjamin. This happened on the eleventh day of the eighth month in the first of the sixth week of this jubilee.

34 Rachel died there and she was buried in the land of Ephrath, the same is Bethlehem, and Jacob built a pillar on the grave of Rachel, on the road above her grave.

[Chapter *33*]

1 Jacob went and lived to the south of Magdaladra'ef. He and Leah, his wife, went to his father, Isaac, on the new moon of the tenth month.

2 Reuben saw Bilhah, Rachel's maid, the concubine of his father, bathing in water in a secret place, and he loved her.

3 He hid himself at night, and he entered the house of Bilhah at night. He found her sleeping alone on a bed in her house.

4 He had sex with her. She awoke and saw that is was Reuben lying with her in the bed. She uncovered the border of her covering and grabbed him and cried out when she discovered that it was Reuben.

5 She was ashamed because of him and released her hand from him, and he fled.

6 Because of this, she mourned greatly and did not tell it to any one.

7 When Jacob returned and sought her, she said to him, "I am not clean for you. I have been defiled in regard to you. Reuben has defiled me, and has had sex with me in the night. I was asleep and did not realize he was there until he uncovered my skirt and had sex with me."

8 Jacob was very angry with Reuben because he had sex with Bilhah, because he had uncovered his father's skirt.

9 Jacob did not approach her again because Reuben had defiled her. And as for any man who uncovers his father's skirt his deed is greatly wicked, for he is disgusting to the Lord.

10 For this reason it is written and ordained on the heavenly tablets that a man should not lie with his father's wife, and should not uncover his father's skirt. This is unclean and they shall surely die together, the man who lies with his father's wife and the woman also, for they have committed uncleanness on the earth.

11 There shall be nothing unclean before our God in the nation that He has chosen for Himself as a possession.

12 Again, it is written a second time, "Cursed be he who lies with the wife of his father, for he has uncovered his father's shame." All the holy ones of the Lord said, "So be it. So be it."

13 "Moses, command the children of Israel so that they observe this word. It entails a punishment of death. It is unclean, and there is no atonement forever for the man who has committed this. He is to be put to death. Kill him by stoning. Root him out from among the people of our God.

14 No man who does so in Israel will be permitted to remain alive a single day on the earth. He is abominable and unclean.

15 Do not let them say, "Reuben was granted life and forgiveness after he had sex with his father's concubine, although she had a husband, and her husband, Jacob, his father, was still alive."

16 Until that time the ordinance and judgment and law had not been revealed in its completeness for all. In your days it has been revealed as a law of seasons and of days. It is an everlasting law for all generations forever. For this law has no limit of days, and no atonement for it.

17 They must both be rooted out of the entire nation. On the day they committed it they shall be killed.

18 Moses, write it down for Israel that they may observe it, and do according to these words, and not commit a sin punishable by death. The Lord our God is judge, who does not respect persons (position) and accepts no gifts.

19 Tell them these words of the covenant, that they may hear and observe, and be on their guard with respect to them, and not be destroyed and rooted out of the land; for an uncleanness, and an abomination, and a contamination, and a pollution are all they who commit it on the earth before our God.

20 There is no greater sin on earth than fornication that they commit. Israel is a holy nation to the Lord its God, and a nation of inheritance. It is a priestly and royal nation and for

His own possession. There shall appear no such uncleanness among the holy nation.

21 In the third year of this sixth week, Jacob and all his sons went and lived in the house of Abraham, near Isaac his father and Rebecca his mother.

22 These were the names of the sons of Jacob, the first-born Reuben, Simeon, Levi, Judah, Issachar, Zebulon, which are the sons of Leah. The sons of Rachel are Joseph and Benjamin. The sons of Bilhah are Dan and Naphtali; and the sons of Zilpah, Gad and Asher. Dinah is the daughter of Leah, the only daughter of Jacob.

23 They came and bowed themselves to Isaac and Rebecca. When they saw them they blessed Jacob and all his sons, and Isaac rejoiced greatly, for he saw the sons of Jacob, his younger son and he blessed them.

[Chapter *34*]

1 In the sixth year of this week of the forty-fourth jubilee Jacob sent his sons and his servants to pasture their sheep in the pastures of Shechem.

2 The seven kings of the Amorites assembled themselves together (to fight) against them and kill them. They hid themselves under the trees, to take their cattle as booty.

3 Jacob, Levi, Judah and Joseph were in the house with Isaac their father, for his spirit was sorrowful, and they could not leave him. Benjamin was the youngest, and for this reason he remained with his father.

4 The king of Taphu, the king of Aresa, the king of Seragan, the king of Selo, the king of Ga'as, the king of Bethoron, the king of Ma'anisakir, and all those who dwell in these mountains and who dwell in the woods in the land of Canaan came.

5 They announced to Jacob saying, "Look, the kings of the Amorites have surrounded your sons, and plundered their herds."

6 And he left his house, he and his three sons and all the servants of his father, and his own servants, and he went against them with six thousand men, who carried swords.

7 He killed them in the pastures of Shechem, and pursued those who fled, and he killed them with the edge of the sword, and he killed Aresa and Taphu and Saregan and Selo and Amani sakir and Gaga'as, and he recovered his herds.

8 He conquered them, and imposed tribute on them that they should pay him five fruit products of their land. He built (the cities of) Robel and Tamnatares.

9 He returned in peace, and made peace with them, and they became his servants until the day that he and his sons went down into Egypt.

10 In the seventh year of this week he sent Joseph from his house to the land of Shechem to learn about the welfare of his brothers. He found them in the land of Dothan.

11 They dealt treacherously with him, and formed a plot against him to kill him, but they changed their minds and sold him to Ishmaelite merchants. They brought him down into Egypt, and they sold him to Potiphar, the eunuch of Pharaoh, the chief of the cooks and priest of the city of Elew."

12 The sons of Jacob slaughtered a kid, and dipped Joseph's coat in the blood and sent it to Jacob their father on the tenth of the seventh month.

13 They brought it to him in the evening and he mourned all that night. He became feverish with mourning for Joseph's death, and he said, "An evil beast has devoured Joseph". All the members of his house mourned and grieved with him that day.

14 His sons and his daughter got up to comfort him, but he refused to be comforted for his son.

15 On that day Bilhah heard that Joseph had perished, and she died mourning him. She was living in Qafratef, and Dinah, his daughter, died after Joseph had perished.

16 There were now three reasons for Israel to mourn in one month. They buried Bilhah next to the tomb of Rachel, and Dinah, his daughter. They were (all) buried there.

17 He mourned for Joseph one year, and did not cease, for he said, "Let me go down to my grave mourning for my son."

18 For this reason it is ordained for the children of Israel that they should remember and mourn on the tenth of the seventh month. On that day the news came which made Jacob weep for Joseph. On this day they should make atonement for their sins for themselves with a young goat on the tenth of the seventh month, once a year, for they had grieved the sorrow of their father regarding Joseph his son.

19 This day, once a year, has been ordained that they should grieve on it for their sins, and for all their transgressions and for all their errors, so that they might cleanse themselves.

20 After Joseph perished, the sons of Jacob took to themselves wives. The name of Reuben's wife is Ada; and the name of Simeon's wife is Adlba'a, a Canaanite. The name of Levi's wife is Melka, of the daughters of Aram, of the offspring of the sons of Terah. The name of Judah's wife is Betasu'el, a Canaanite. The name of Issachar's wife is Hezaqa, and the name of Zabulon's wife is Ni'iman. The name of Dan's wife is Egla. The name of Naphtali's wife is Rasu'u, of Mesopotamia. The name of Gad's wife is Maka. The name of Asher's wife is Ijona. The name of Joseph's wife is Asenath, the Egyptian. The name of Benjamin's wife is Ijasaka.

21 And Simeon repented, and took a second wife from Mesopotamia as his brothers had done.

[Chapter 35]

1 In the first year of the first week of the forty-fifth jubilee Rebecca called Jacob, her son, and commanded him regarding his father and regarding his brother, that he should honor them all the days of his life.

2 Jacob said, "I will do everything you have commanded. I will honor them. This will be honor and greatness to me, and righteousness before the Lord.

3 Mother, you know from the time I was born until this day, all my deeds and all that is in my heart. I always think good concerning all.

4 Why should I not do this thing which you have commanded me, that I should honor my father and my brother?

5 Tell me, mother, what perversity have you seen in me and I shall turn away from it, and mercy will be on me."

6 She said to him, "My son, in all my days I have not seen any perverseness in you, but only upright deeds. Yet, I will tell you the truth, my son, I shall die this year. I shall not survive this year in my life. I have seen the day of my death in a dream. I should not live beyond a hundred and fifty-five years. I have completed all the days that I am to live my life."

7 Jacob laughed at the words of his mother because his mother had said she should die. She was sitting across from him in possession of her strength, and she was still strong.

She came and went (as she wished). She could see well, and her teeth were strong. No sickness had touched her all the days of her life.

8 Jacob said to her, "If my days of life are close to yours and my strength remains with me as your strength has, I would be blessed, mother. You will not die. You are simply joking with me regarding your death."

9 She went in to Isaac and said to him, " I make one request of you. Make Esau swear that he will not injure Jacob, nor pursue him with intent to harm him. You know Esau's thoughts have been perverse from his youth, and there is no goodness in him. He desires to kill him after you die.

10 You know all that he has done since the day Jacob, his brother, went to Haran until this day. He has forsaken us with his whole heart, and has done evil to us. He has stolen your flocks and carried off all your possessions while you watched.

11 When we asked him and begged him for what was our own, he did as a man (stranger) who was taking pity on us (giving a token like one giving alms to a beggar).

12 He is bitter against you because you blessed Jacob, your perfect and upright son. There is no evil but only goodness in Jacob. Since he came from Haran to this day he has not robbed us of anything. He always brings us everything in its season. He rejoices and blesses us with all his heart when we take his hands. He has not parted from us since he came from Haran until this day, and he remains with us continually at home honoring us."

13 Isaac said to her, "I also know and see the deeds of Jacob who is with us, how he honors us with all his heart. Before, I loved Esau more than Jacob because he was the first-born, but now I love Jacob more than Esau, for Esau has done many evil deeds, and there is no righteousness in him. All his ways are unrighteousness and violence.

14 My heart is troubled because of all his deeds. Neither he nor his offspring will be exempt because they are those who will be destroyed from the earth and who will be rooted out from under heaven. He and his children have forsaken the God of Abraham and gone after his wives (wives' gods) and after their uncleanness and after their error.

15 You told me to make him swear that he will not kill Jacob his brother, but even if he swears, he will not abide by his oath. He will not do good but evil only.

16 If he desires to kill Jacob, his brother, then into Jacob's hands he will be given. He will not escape from Jacob's hands.

17 Do not be afraid for Jacob, for the guardian of Jacob is great, powerful, honored, and praised more than the guardian of Esau."

18 Rebecca called for Esau and he came to her, and she said to him, "I have a request of you, my son. Promise to do it, my son."

19 He said, "I will do everything that you say to me, and I will not refuse your request."

20 She said to him, "I ask you that the day I die, you will take me in and bury me near Sarah, your father's mother, and that you and Jacob will love each other and that neither will desire evil against the other, but (have) mutual love only. Do this so you will prosper, my son, and be honored in the all of the land, and no enemy will rejoice over you. You will be a blessing and a mercy in the eyes of all those that love you."

21 He said, "I will do all that you have told me. I shall bury you on the day you die near Sarah, my father's mother, as you have desired that her bones may be near your bones.

22 Jacob, my brother, I shall love above all flesh. I have only one brother in all the earth but him. It is only what is expected of me. It is no great thing if I love him, for he is my brother, and we were sown together in your body, and together came we out from your womb. If I do not love my brother, whom shall I love?

23 I beg you to exhort Jacob concerning me and concerning my sons, for I know that he will assuredly be king over me and my sons, for on the day my father blessed him he made him the higher and me the lower.

24 I swear to you that I shall love him, and not desire evil against him all the days of my life but good only."

25 And he swore to her regarding all this matter. While Esau was there, she called Jacob and gave him her orders according to the words that she had spoken to Esau.

26 He said, "I shall do your pleasure, believe me that no evil will proceed from me or from my sons against Esau. I shall be first in nothing except in love only."

27 She and her sons ate and drank that night, and she died, three jubilees and one week and one year old on that night. Her two sons, Esau and Jacob, buried her in the double cave near Sarah, their father's mother.

[Chapter *36*]

1 In the sixth year of this week Isaac called his two sons Esau and Jacob, and they came to him, and he said to them, "My sons, I am going the way of my fathers, to the eternal house where my fathers are.

2 Bury me near Abraham my father, in the double cave in the field of Ephron the Hittite, where Abraham purchased a sepulcher to bury in. Bury me in the sepulcher I dug for myself.

3 I command you, my sons, to practice righteousness and uprightness on the earth, so that the Lord may do to you what he said he would do to Abraham and to his offspring.

4 Love one another. Love your brothers as a man who loves his own soul. Let each seek how he may benefit his brother, and act together on the earth. Let them love each other as their own souls.

5 I command and warn you to reject idols. Hate them, and do not love them. They are fully deceptive to those that worship them and for those that bow down to them.

6 Remember the Lord God of Abraham, your father, and how I worshipped Him and served Him in righteousness and in joy, that God might multiply you and increase your offspring as the multitude of stars in heaven, and establish you on the earth as the plant of righteousness, which will not be rooted out to all the generations forever.

7 And now I shall make you swear a great oath, for there is no oath which is greater than that which is by the name glorious, honored, great, splendid, wonderful and mighty, which created the heavens and the earth and all things together, that you will fear Him and worship Him.

8 Each will love his brother with affection and righteousness. Neither will desire to do evil against his brother from now on forever all the days of your life so that you may prosper in all your deeds and not be destroyed.

9 If either of you plans evil against his brother, know that he that plans evil shall fall into his brother's hand, and shall be rooted out of the land of the living, and his offspring shall be destroyed from under heaven.

10 But on that day there will be turbulence, curses, wrath, anger, and will He burn his land and his city and all that is his with a devouring fire like the fire He sent to burn Sodom and he shall be blotted out of the book of the discipline of the children of men, and he will not be recorded in the book of life. He shall be added in the book of destruction. He shall depart into eternal curses. Their condemnation may be always renewed in hate and in curses and in wrath and in torment and in anger and in plagues and in disease forever.

11 My sons, this, I say and testify to you, will be the result according to the judgment which shall come on the man who wishes to injure his brother."

12 Then he divided all his possessions between the two on that day, and he gave the larger portion to him that was the first-born, and the tower and all that was around it, and all that Abraham possessed at the Well of the Oath.

13 He said, "This larger portion I will give to the first-born."

14 Esau said, "I have sold and relinquished my birthright to Jacob. Let it be given to him. I have nothing to say regarding it, for it is his."

15 Isaac said, "May a blessing rest on you, my sons, and on your offspring this day. You have given me rest, and my heart is not pained concerning the birthright, or that you should work wickedness because of it.

16 May the Most High God bless the man and his offspring forever that does righteousness."

17 He stopped commanding them and blessing them, and they ate and drank together in front of him, and he rejoiced because there was one mind between them, and they went out from him and rested that day and slept.

18 Isaac slept on his bed that day rejoicing. He slept the eternal sleep, and died one hundred and eighty years old. He lived twenty-five weeks and five years; and his two sons, Esau and Jacob, buried him.

19 After that Esau went to the land of Edom, to the mountains of Seir, and lived there.

20 Jacob lived in the mountains of Hebron, in the high place of the land in which his father Abraham had journeyed. He worshipped the Lord with all his heart. He had divided the days of his generations according to the commands he had seen.

21 Leah, his wife, died in the fourth year of the second week of the forty-fifth jubilee, and he buried her in the double cave near Rebecca his mother to the left of the grave of Sarah, his father's mother. All her sons and his sons came to mourn over Leah, his wife, with him and to comfort him regarding her. He was lamenting her for he loved her greatly after Rachel, her sister, died. She was perfect and upright in all her ways and she honored Jacob. All the days that she lived with him he did not hear from her mouth a harsh word, for she was gentle, peaceable, upright and honorable.

22 And he remembered all the deeds she had done during her life and he lamented her greatly. He loved her with all his heart and with all his soul.

[Chapter *37*]

1 On the day that Isaac, the father of Jacob and Esau died, the sons of Esau heard that Isaac had given the elder's portion to his younger son, Jacob, and they were very angry.

2 They argued with their father, saying, "Why has your father given Jacob the portion of the elder and passed you over even though you are the elder and Jacob the younger?"

3 He said to them, "Because I sold my birthright to Jacob for a small portion of lentils (lentil soup), and on the day my father sent me to hunt, catch, and bring him something that he should eat and bless me, Jacob came with deceit and brought my father food and drink. My father blessed him and put me under his hand.

4 Now our father has caused Jacob and me to swear that we shall not devise evil plans against his brother (each other), and that we shall continue in love and in peace each with his brother and not make our ways corrupt."

5 They said to him, "We shall not listen to you to make peace with him. We are stronger than him and we are more powerful than he is. We shall depose him and kill him, and destroy him and his sons. If you will not go with us, we shall hurt you also.

6 Listen! Let us send to Aram, Philistia, Moab, and Ammon. Let us take chosen men who are trained in battle, and let us go against him and do battle with him. Let us exterminate him from the earth before he grows strong."

7 Their father said to them, "Do not go and do not make war with him or you shall fall before him."

8 They said to him, "This is how you have acted from your youth until this day. You have continued to put your neck under his yoke. We shall not listen to these words."

9 Then they sent to Aram, and to Aduram to the friend of their father, and they also hired one thousand chosen men of war.

10 And there came to them from Moab and from the children of Ammon, those who were hired, one thousand chosen men, and from Philistia, one thousand chosen warriors, and from Edom and from the Horites one thousand chosen warriors, and from the Kittim mighty warriors.

11 They said to their father, "Go out with them and lead them or else we shall kill you."

12 And he was filled with boiling anger on seeing that his sons were forcing him to go before them to lead them against Jacob, his brother.

13 But afterward he remembered all the evil that lay hidden in his heart against Jacob his brother, and he did not remember the oath he had sworn to his father and to his mother that he would plan no evil against Jacob, his brother, all his days.

14 Because Jacob was in mourning for his wife Leah, he did not know they were coming to battle against him until they approached the tower with four thousand soldiers and chosen warriors. The men of Hebron sent to him saying, "Look your brother has come against you to fight. He has with him four thousand men carrying swords, shields, and weapons." They told him this because they loved Jacob more than Esau.

15 So they told him, for Jacob was a more gracious and merciful man than Esau.

16 But Jacob would not believe until they came very near to the tower.

17 He closed the gates of the tower; and he stood on the battlements and spoke to his brother Esau and said, "Noble is the comfort you have come to give me concerning the death of my wife. Is this the oath that you swore to your father and again to your mother before they died? You have broken the oath, and on the moment that you swore to your father you were condemned."

18 Then Esau answered and said to him, "Neither the children of men nor the beasts of the earth have sworn an oath of righteousness and kept it forever. Every day they lay evil plans one against another regarding how they might kill their adversary or foe.

19 You will hate my children and me forever, so there is no observing the tie of brotherhood with you.

20 Hear these words that I declare to you. If the boar can change its skin and make its bristles as soft as wool, or if it can cause horns to sprout out on its head like the horns of a stag or of a sheep, then will I observe the tie of brotherhood with you. Like breasts separate themselves from their mother (and fight), you and I have never been brothers.

21 If the wolves make peace with the lambs and not devour or do them violence, and if their hearts are towards them for good, then there shall be peace in my heart towards you. If the lion becomes the friend of the ox and makes peace with him and if he is bound under one yoke with him and plows with him, then will I make peace with you.

22 When the raven becomes white as the raza (a white bird?), then know that I have loved you and shall make peace with you. You will be rooted out, and your sons shall be rooted out, and there shall be no peace for you."

23 Jacob saw that Esau had decided in his heart to do evil toward him, and that he desired with all his soul to kill him. Jacob saw that Esau had come pouncing like the wild boar which charges the spear that is set to pierce and kill it, and yet does not even slow down. Then he spoke to his own people and to his servants and told them that Esau and his men were going to attack him and all his companions.

[Chapter *38*]

1 After that Judah spoke to Jacob, his father, and said to him, "Bend your bow, father, and send forth your arrows and bring down the adversary and kill the enemy. You have the power to do it. We will not kill your brother because he is your kin and he is like you, so we will honor his life."

2 Then Jacob bent his bow and sent forth the arrow and struck Esau, his brother, on the right side of his chest and killed him.

3 And again he sent forth an arrow and struck Adoran the Aramaean, on the left side of his chest, and it drove him backward and killed him. Then the sons of Jacob and their servants went out, dividing themselves into companies on the four sides of the tower.

4 Judah went out in front. Naphtali and Gad along with fifty servants went to the south side of the tower, and they killed all they found before them. Not one individual escaped.

5 Levi, Dan, and Asher went out on the east side of the tower along with fifty men, and they killed the warriors of Moab and Ammon.

6 Reuben, Issachar, and Zebulon went out on the north side of the tower along with fifty men and they killed the warriors of the Philistines.

7 Reuben's son, Simeon, Benjamin, and Enoch went out on the west side of the tower along with fifty men and they killed four hundred men, stout warriors of Edom and of the Horites. Six hundred fled, and four of the sons of Esau fled with them, and left their father lying killed, as he had fallen on the hill that is in Aduram.

8 And the sons of Jacob pursued them to the mountains of Seir. And Jacob buried his brother on the hill that is in Aduram, and he returned to his house.

9 The sons of Jacob crushed the sons of Esau in the mountains of Seir, and made them bow their necks so that they became servants of the sons of Jacob.

10 They sent a message to their father to inquire whether they should make peace with them or kill them.

11 Jacob sent word to his sons that they should make peace. They made peace with them but also placed the yoke of servitude on them, so that they paid tribute to Jacob and to his sons always.

12 And they continued to pay tribute to Jacob until the day that he went down to Egypt.

13 The sons of Edom have not escaped the yoke of servitude imposed by the twelve sons of Jacob until this day.

14 These are the kings that reigned in Edom before there was any king over the children of Israel (until this day) in the land of Edom.

15 And Balaq, the son of Beor, reigned in Edom, and the name of his city was Danaba. Balaq died, and Jobab, the son of Zara of Boser, ruled in his place.

16 Jobab died, and Asam, of the land of Teman, ruled in his place.

17 Asam died, and Adath, the son of Barad, who killed Midian in the field of Moab, ruled in his place, and the name of his city was Avith.

18 Adath died, and Salman, from Amaseqa, ruled in his place.

19 Salman died, and Saul of Ra'aboth by the river, ruled in his place. Saul died, and Ba'elunan, the son of Achbor, ruled in his place.

20 Ba'elunan, the son of Achbor died, and Adath ruled in his place, and the name of his wife was Maitabith, the daughter of Matarat, the daughter of Metabedza'ab. These are the kings who reigned in the land of Edom.

[Chapter *39*]

1 Jacob lived in the land that his father journeyed in, which is the land of Canaan.

2 These are the generations of Jacob. Joseph was seventeen years old when they took him down into the land of Egypt, and Potiphar, a eunuch of Pharaoh, the chief cook, bought him.

3 He made Joseph the manager over Potiphar's entire house and the blessing of the Lord came on the house of the Egyptian because of Joseph. And the Lord caused him to prosper in all that he did.

4 The Egyptian turned everything over to the hands of Joseph because he saw that the Lord was with him, and that the Lord caused him to prosper him in all that he did.

5 Joseph's appearance was beautiful, and his master's wife watched Joseph, and she loved him and wanted him to have sex with her.

6 But he did not surrender his soul because he remembered the Lord and the words which Jacob, his father, used to read to him from the writings of Abraham, that no man should commit fornication with a woman who has a husband. For him the punishment of death has been ordained in the heavens before the Most High God, and the sin will be recorded against him in the eternal books, which are always in the presence of the Lord.

7 Joseph remembered these words and refused to have sex with her.

8 And she begged him for a year, but he refused and would not listen.

9 But while he was in the house she embraced him and held him tightly in order to force him to sleep with her. She closed the doors of the house and held on to him, but he left his garment in her hands and broke through the door and ran out from her presence.

10 The woman saw that he would not sleep with her, and she slandered him in the presence of his master, saying "Your Hebrew servant, whom you love, sought to force me to have sex with him. When I shouted for help he fled and left his garment in my hands. I tried to stop him but he broke through the door."

11 When the Egyptian saw Joseph's garment and the broken door, and heard the words of his wife, he threw Joseph into prison and put him in the place where the prisoners of the king were kept.

12 He was there in the prison, and the Lord gave Joseph favor in the sight of the chief of the prison guards and caused him to have compassion for Joseph, because he saw that the Lord was with him, and that the Lord made all that he did to prosper.

13 He turned over all things into his hands, and the chief of the prison guards knew of nothing that was going on in the prison, because Joseph did everything for him, and the Lord perfected it. He remained there two years.

14 In those days Pharaoh, king of Egypt, was very angry at his two eunuchs, the chief butler, and the chief baker. He put them in the prison facility of the house of the chief cook, where Joseph was kept.

15 The chief of the prison guards appointed Joseph to serve them, and he served them.

16 They both dreamed a dream, the chief butler and the chief baker, and they told it to Joseph.

17 As he interpreted to them so it happened to them, and Pharaoh restored the chief butler to his office and he killed the chief baker as Joseph had interpreted to them.

18 But the chief butler forgot Joseph was in the prison, although he had informed him of what would happen to him. He did not remember to inform Pharaoh of how Joseph had told him (about his dream), because he forgot.

[Chapter *40*]

1 In those days Pharaoh dreamed two dreams in one night concerning a famine that was to be in all the land, and he awoke from his sleep and called all the magicians and interpreters of dreams that were in Egypt. He told them his two dreams but they were not able to tell him what they meant.

2 Then the chief butler remembered Joseph and told the king of him, and he brought him out from the prison, and the king told his two dreams to him.

3 He said before Pharaoh that his two dreams were one, and he said to him, "Seven years shall come in which there shall be plenty in all the land of Egypt, but after that, seven years of famine. Such a famine as has not been in all the land.

4 Now, let Pharaoh appoint administrators in all the land of Egypt, and let them store up food in every city throughout all the years of plenty, and there will be food for the seven years of famine, and those of the land will not perish through the famine, even though it will be very severe."

5 The Lord gave Joseph favor and mercy in the eyes of Pharaoh. Pharaoh said to his servants, "We shall not find such a wise and prudent man like this man, because the spirit of the Lord is with him."

6 And he appointed Joseph the second in command in his entire kingdom and gave him authority over all Egypt, and placed him on the second chariot of Pharaoh to ride.

7 And he clothed him with fine linen clothes, and he put a gold chain around his neck, and a crier proclaimed before him "El" "El wa Abirer," and he placed a ring on his hand and made him ruler over all his house, and lifted him up before the people, and said to him, "Only on the throne shall I be greater than you."

8 Joseph ruled over all the land of Egypt, and all the governors of Pharaoh, and all his servants, and all those who did the king's business loved him because he walked in uprightness, because he was without pride and arrogance. He did not judge people by their position, and did not accept gifts, but he judged all the people of the land in uprightness.

9 The land of Egypt was at peace before Pharaoh because of Joseph, because the Lord was with him, and the Lord gave him favor and mercy for all his generations before all those who knew him and those who heard of him, and Pharaoh's kingdom was run efficiently, and there was no Satan (adversary) and no evil person in it.

10 And the king called Joseph's name Sephantiphans, and gave Joseph the daughter of Potiphar, the daughter of the priest of Heliopolis, the chief cook to marry.

11 On the day that Joseph stood before Pharaoh he was thirty years old.

12 In that year Isaac died. Things transpired as Joseph had said in the interpretation of Pharaoh's dream and there were seven years of plenty over all the land of Egypt, and the land of Egypt abundantly produced, one measure producing eighteen hundred measures.

13 Joseph gathered food into every city until they were full of grain and they could no longer count or measure it because of its multitude.

[Chapter *41*]

1 In the forty-fifth jubilee, in the second week, and in the second year, Judah took his first-born Er, a wife from the daughters of Aram, named Tamar.

2 But he hated her, and did not have sex with her, because her mother was of the daughters of Canaan, and he wished to take him a wife of the lineage of his mother, but Judah, his father, would not permit him to do that.

3 Er, the first-born of Judah, was wicked, and the Lord killed him.

4 And Judah said to Onan, his brother, "Go in to your brother's wife and perform the duty of a husband's brother to her, and raise up offspring to your brother."

5 Onan knew that the offspring would not be his, but his brother's only, and he went into the house of his brother's wife, and spilt his seed (ejaculates) on the ground, and he was wicked in the eyes of the Lord, and He killed him.

6 Judah said to Tamar, his daughter-in-law, "Remain in your father's house as a widow until Shelah, my son has grown up, and I shall give you to him to wife."

7 He grew up, but Bedsu'el, the wife of Judah, did not permit her son Shelah to marry. Bedsu'el, Judah's wife, died in the fifth year of this week.

8 In the sixth year Judah went up to shear his sheep at Timnah.

9 And they told Tamar, "Look, your father-in-law is going up to Timnah to shear his sheep." And she took off her widow's clothes, and put on a veil, and adorned herself, and sat in the gate connecting the road to Timnah.

10 As Judah was going along he saw her, and thought she was a prostitute, and he said to her, "Let me come in to you," and she said to him, "Come in," and he went in.

11 She said to him, "Give me my pay," and he said to her, "I have nothing with me except my ring that is on my finger, my necklace, and my staff which is in my hand."

12 She said to him, "Give them to me until you send me my pay." And he said to her, "I will send to you a kid of the goats", and he gave her his ring, necklace, and staff, and she conceived by him.

13 Judah went to his sheep, and she went to her father's house.

14 Judah sent a kid of the goats by the hand of his shepherd, an Adullamite, but he could not find her, so he asked the people of the place, saying, "Where is the prostitute who was here?"

15 They said to him, "There is no prostitute here with us." And he returned and informed Judah that he had not found her, "I asked the people of the place, and they said to me, "There is no prostitute here." "

16 He said, "If you see her give the kids to her or we become a cause of ridicule." And when she had completed three months, it was revealed that she was with child, and they told Judah, saying, "Look Tamar, your daughter-in-law, is with child by whoredom."

17 And Judah went to the house of her father, and said to her father and her brothers, "Bring her out, and let them burn her, for she has committed uncleanness in Israel."

18 It happened when they brought her out to burn her that she sent to her father-in-law the ring and the necklace, and the staff, saying, "Tell us whose are these, because by him am I with child."

19 Judah acknowledged, and said, "Tamar is more righteous than I am.

20 Do not let them burn her." For that reason she was not given to Shelah, and he did not again approach her and after that she gave birth to two sons, Perez and Zerah, in the seventh year of this second week.

21 At this time the seven years of fruitfulness were completed, of which Joseph spoke to Pharaoh.

22 Judah acknowledged the evil deed that he had done because he had sex with his daughter-in-law, and he hated himself for it.

23 He acknowledged that he had transgressed and gone astray, because he had uncovered the skirt of his son, and he began to lament and to supplicate before the Lord because of his transgression.

24 We told him in a dream that it was forgiven him because he supplicated earnestly, and lamented, and did not commit the act again.

25 And he received forgiveness because he turned from his sin and from his ignorance, because he transgressed greatly before our God. Every one that acts like this, every one who has sex with his mother-in-law, let them burn him alive with fire. Because there is uncleanness and pollution on them, let them burn them alive.

26 Command the children of Israel that there should be no uncleanness among them, because every one who has sex with his daughter-in-law or with his mother-in-law has committed uncleanness. Let them burn the man who has had sex with her with fire, and likewise burn the woman, so that God will turn away wrath and punishment from Israel.

27 We told Judah that his two sons had not had sex with her, and for this reason his offspring was established for a second generation, and would not be rooted out.

28 For in single-mindedness he had gone and sought for punishment, namely, according to the judgment of Abraham, which he had commanded his sons. Judah had sought to burn her alive.

[Chapter *42*]

1 In the first year of the third week of the forty-fifth jubilee the famine began to come into the land, and the rain refused to be given to the earth. None whatsoever fell.

2 The earth became barren, but in the land of Egypt there was food, because Joseph had gathered the seed of the land in the seven years of plenty and had preserved it.

3 The Egyptians came to Joseph that he might give them food, and he opened the storehouses where the grain of the first year was stored, and he sold it to the people of the land for gold.

4 Jacob heard there was food in Egypt, and he sent his ten sons that they should procure food for him in Egypt, and they arrived among those that went there, but Benjamin he did not send.

5 Joseph recognized them, but they did not recognize him. He spoke to them and questioned them, and he said to them, "Are you not spies and have you not come to explore ways to enter this land?"

6 And he put them in custody.

7 After that, he set them free again, and detained Simeon alone and sent his nine brothers away.

8 He filled their sacks with corn, and he put their gold back in their sacks, and they did not know it. Joseph then commanded them to bring their younger brother, because they had told him their father was living and also their younger brother.

9 They went up from the land of Egypt and they came to the land of Canaan. There they told their father all that had happened to them, and how the ruler of the country had spoken rudely to them, and had seized Simeon until they should bring Benjamin.

10 Jacob said, "You have taken my children from me! Joseph is gone and Simeon also is gone, and now you will take Benjamin away. I am the victim of your wickedness."

11 He said, "My son will not go down with you because fate may have it that he would fall sick. Their mother gave birth to two sons, and one has died, and this one also you will take from me. If, by fate, he took a fever on the road, you would turn my old age to sorrow and death."

12 He saw that every man's money had been returned to him in his sack, and for this reason he feared to send him.

13 The famine increased and became grievous in the land of Canaan, and in all lands except in the land of Egypt. Egypt had food because many of the children of the Egyptians had stored up their seed for food from the time when they saw Joseph gathering seed together and putting it in storehouses and preserving it for the years of famine.

14 The people of Egypt fed themselves on it during the first year of their famine but when Israel saw that the famine was very serious in the land, and that there was no deliverance, he said to his sons, "Go again, and procure food for us so that we will not die."

15 They said, "We shall not go unless our youngest brother go with us!"

16 Israel saw that if he did not send Benjamin with them, they would all perish because of the famine.

17 Reuben said, "Give him to me, and if I do not bring him back to you, kill my two sons in payment for his soul." Israel said to Reuben, "He shall not go with you."

18 Judah came near and said, "Send him with me, and if I do not bring him back to you, let me bear your blame all the days of my life."

19 He sent him with them in the second year of this week on the first day of the month.

20 They all came to the land of Egypt, and they had presents in their hands of sweet spice, almonds, turpentine nuts, and pure honey.

21 And they went and stood before Joseph, and he saw Benjamin his brother, and he knew him, and said to them, "Is this your youngest brother?" They said to him, "It is he."

22 He said, "The Lord be gracious to you, my son!" And he sent Benjamin into his house and he brought out Simeon to them. Joseph made a feast for them, and they presented to him the gifts that they had brought in their hands.

23 They ate before Joseph and he gave them all a portion of food, but the portion of food given to Benjamin was seven times larger than any of theirs.

24 And they ate and drank and got up and remained with their donkeys.

25 Joseph devised a plan whereby he might learn their thoughts as to whether they desired peace or not. He said to the steward who was over his house, "Fill all their sacks with food. Place their money back in their vessels. Put my cup, the silver cup out of which I drink, in the sack of the youngest and send them away."

[Chapter *43*]

1 He did as Joseph had told him, and filled all their sacks with food for them and put their money back into their sacks, and put the cup in Benjamin's sack.

2 Early in the morning they departed, and it happened that when they had gone from that place, Joseph said to the steward of his house, "Pursue them, run and seize them, and say, 'You have repaid my kindness with evil. You have stolen from me the silver cup out of which my lord drinks.'

3 Bring me back their youngest brother. Go! Get him quickly before I go to my seat of judgment (judge you guilt of disobeying an order). "

4 He ran after them and said the words as he was told. They said to him, "God forbid that your servants should do this thing, and steal any utensil or money from the house of your lord, like the things we found in our sacks the first time we, your servants, came back from the land of Canaan.

5 We have not stolen any utensil. How could we? Look here in our sacks and search, and wherever you find the cup in the sack of any man among us, let him be killed, and we and our donkeys will serve your lord."

6 He said to them, "Not so. If I find it, the man whose sack I find it in I shall take as a servant, and the rest of you shall return in peace to your house."

7 He was searching in their vessels, beginning with the eldest and ending with the youngest, when it was found in Benjamin's sack.

8 They ripped their garments in frustration, and placed their belongings back on their donkeys, and returned to the city and came to the house of Joseph. They all bowed themselves with their faces to the ground in front of him.

9 Joseph said to them, "You have done evil." They said, "What shall we say and how shall we defend ourselves? Our lord has discovered the transgression of his servants; and now we and our donkeys are the servants of our lord."

10 Joseph said to them, "I too fear the Lord. As for you, go to your homes and let your brother be my servant, because you have done evil. I delight in this cup as no one else delights in his cup and yet you have stolen it from me."

11 Judah said, "O my lord, I pray you to let your servant speak a word in my lord's ear. Your servant's mother had two sons for our father. One went away and was lost, and has not been found since. This one alone is left of his mother, and your servant our father loves him. He would die if the lad were lost to him.

12 When we go to your servant our father, and the lad is not with us, it will happen that he will die. We will have brought so much sorrow on our father it will bring his death.

13 Now rather let me, your servant, stay here as a bondsman to my lord instead of the boy. Let the lad go with his brothers, because I will stand in for him at the hand of your servant our father. If I do not bring him back, your servant will bear the blame of our father forever."

14 Joseph saw that they were all in accord in doing good to one another. Then, he could not refrain himself, and he told them that he was Joseph.

15 And he conversed with them in the Hebrew tongue and hugged their necks and wept.

16 At first they did not recognize him and then they began to weep. He said to them, "Do not weep for me, but hurry and bring my father to me. See, it is my mouth that speaks and the eyes of my brother Benjamin see me.

17 Pay attention. This is the second year of the famine, and there are still five years to come without harvest or fruit of trees or plowing.

18 You and your households come down quickly, so that you won't die because of the famine. Do not be grieved for your possessions, because the Lord sent me before you to set things in order that many people might live.

19 Tell my father that I am still alive. You see that the Lord has made me as a father to Pharaoh, and ruler over his house and over all the land of Egypt.

20 Tell my father of all my glory, and all the riches and glory that the Lord has given me."

21 By the command of Pharaoh's mouth, he gave them chariots and provisions for the way, and he gave them all multi-colored raiment and silver.

22 He sent corn, raiment, silver, and ten donkeys that carried all of this to his father, and he sent them away.

23 They went up and told their father that Joseph was alive, and was measuring out corn to all the nations of the earth, and that he was ruler over all the land of Egypt.

24 But their father did not believe it, because he was not in his right mind. But when he saw the wagons, which Joseph had sent, the life of his spirit revived, and he said, "It is enough for me if Joseph lives. I will go down and see him before I die."

[Chapter *44*]

1 Israel took his journey from Haran's house on the new moon of the third month, and he stopped at the Well of the Oath on the way and he offered a sacrifice to the God of his father Isaac on the seventh of this month.

2 Jacob remembered the dream that he had at Bethel, and he feared to go down into Egypt.

3 He was thinking of sending word to Joseph to come to him because he did not want to go down. He remained there seven days, hoping fate would permit him to see a vision as to whether he should remain or go down.

4 He celebrated the harvest festival of the first-fruits with old grain, because in all the land of Canaan there was not a handful of seed in the ground because the famine was affecting all the beasts, and cattle, and birds, and all men.

5 On the sixteenth the Lord appeared to him, and said to him, "Jacob, Jacob," and he said, "Here I am."

6 And He said to him, "I am the God of your fathers, the God of Abraham and Isaac. Do not be afraid to go down into Egypt, because I will be there to make you a great nation. I will go down with you, and I will bring you up again. You will be buried in this land and Joseph will put his hands on your eyes (to close them in death). Do not be afraid. Go down into Egypt."

7 And his sons got up and placed their father and their possessions on wagons.

8 Israel got up from the Well of the Oath on the sixteenth of this third month, and he went to the land of Egypt.

9 Israel sent Judah before him to his son Joseph to examine the Land of Goshen, because Joseph had told his brothers that they should come and live there so they could be near him.

10 This was the best land in Egypt. It was near to him and suitable for all of the cattle they had.

11 These are the names of the sons of Jacob who went into Egypt with Jacob their father; Reuben, the First-born of Israel and his sons Enoch, and Pallu, and Hezron and Carmi, making five.

12 Simeon and his sons Jemuel, and Jamin, and Ohad, and Jachin, and Zohar, and Shaul, the son of the Zephathite woman, making seven.

13 Levi and his sons Gershon, and Kohath, and Merari, making four.

14 Judah and his sons Shela, and Perez, and Zerah, making four.

15 Issachar and his sons Tola, and Phua, and Jasub, and Shimron, making five.

16 Zebulon and his sons Sered, and Elon, and Jahleel, making four.

17 These are the sons of Jacob and their sons whom Leah bore to Jacob in Mesopotamia, six, and their one sister, Dinah and all the souls of the sons of Leah, and their sons, who went with Jacob their father into Egypt. Twenty-nine souls, and Jacob, making thirty, were the number of people that went into Egypt.

18 And the sons of Zilpah, Leah's handmaid, the wife of Jacob, who bore to Jacob Gad and Ashur and their sons who went with him into Egypt.

19 The sons of Gad are Ziphion, and Haggi, and Shuni, and Ezbon, and Eri, and Areli, and Arodi, which make eight souls in total. The sons of Asher are Imnah, and Ishvah, and Ishvi, and Beriah, and Serah, and their one sister, which makes six in total.

20 All the souls were fourteen, and all those of Leah were forty-four.

21 The sons of Rachel, the wife of Jacob are Joseph and Benjamin.

22 There were born to Joseph in Egypt before his father came into Egypt, those whom Asenath, daughter of Potiphar, priest of Heliopolis gave birth to him, Manasseh, and Ephraim. The wife and children of Joseph totaled three.

23 The sons of Benjamin, Bela and Becher and Ashbel, Gera, and Naaman, and Ehi, and Rosh, and Muppim, and Huppim, and Ard with Benjamin totaled eleven.

24 And all the souls of Rachel were fourteen.

25 And the sons of Bilhah, the handmaid of Rachel, the wife of Jacob, whom she gave birth to Jacob, were Dan and Naphtali. These are the names of their sons who went with them into Egypt.

26 The sons of Dan were Hushim, and Samon, and Asudi. and "Ijaka, and Salomon, all totaling six.

27 All but one died the year in which they entered into Egypt, and there was left to Dan only Hushim.

28 These are the names of the sons of Naphtali: Jahziel, and Guni and Jezer, and Shallum, and 'Iv.

29 And 'Iv, who was born after the years of famine, died in Egypt.

30 All the souls (offspring) of Rachel were twenty-six.

31 All the souls (offspring) of Jacob, which went into Egypt, were seventy souls.

32 These are his children and his children's children, in all seventy, but five died in Egypt in the time of Joseph's rule and they had no children.

33 In the land of Canaan two sons of Judah died, Er and Onan, and they had no children, and the children of Israel buried those who died, and they were counted among the seventy Gentile nations.

[Chapter *45*]

1 On the new moon of the fourth month, in the second year of the third week of the forty-fifth jubilee, Israel went into the country of Egypt, to the land of Goshen.

2 Joseph went to meet his father, Jacob, in the land of Goshen, and he hugged his father's neck and wept.

3 Israel said to Joseph, "Now that I have seen you let me die and may the Lord God of Israel, the God of Abraham, and the God of Isaac, who has not withheld His mercy and His grace from His servant Jacob, be blessed.

4 It is enough for me to have seen your face while I am yet alive. Yes, this is the true vision which I saw at Bethel.

5 Blessed be the Lord my God forever and ever, and blessed be His name."

6 Joseph and his brothers ate bread in the presence of their father and drank wine, and Jacob rejoiced with very great joy because he saw Joseph eating with his brothers and drinking in the presence of him, and he blessed the Creator of all things who had preserved him, and had preserved for him his twelve sons.

7 Joseph had given his father and his brothers as a gift the right of dwelling in the land of Goshen and in Rameses and the entire region around it, which he ruled over in the presence of Pharaoh.

8 Israel and his sons dwelt in the land of Goshen, the best part of the land of Egypt, and Israel was one hundred and thirty years old when he came into Egypt. Joseph nourished his father and his brothers and also their possessions (servants) with bread as much as they needed for the seven years of the famine.

9 The land of Egypt became available for purchase because of the famine, and Joseph acquired all the land of Egypt for Pharaoh in return for food, and he got possession of the people and their cattle and everything for Pharaoh.

10 The years of the famine were completed, and Joseph gave the people in the land seed and food that they might sow the land in the eighth year, because the river had overflowed all the land of Egypt.

11 For in the seven years of the famine it had not overflowed and had irrigated only a few places on the banks of the river, but now it overflowed and the Egyptians sowed the land, and it produced much corn that year.

12 This was the first year of the fourth week of the forty-fifth jubilee. Joseph took one-fifth of the corn of the harvest for the king and left four parts for them for food and for seed, and Joseph made it a law for Egypt until this day.

13 Israel lived in the land of Egypt seventeen years, and all the days which he lived were three jubilees, one hundred and forty-seven years, and he died in the fourth year of the fifth week of the forty-fifth jubilee.

14 Israel blessed his sons before he died and told them everything that they would go through in the land of Egypt. He revealed to them what they would live through in the last days, and he blessed them and gave Joseph two portions of the land.

15 He slept with his fathers, and he was buried in the double cave in the land of Canaan, near Abraham his father, in the grave which he dug for himself in the land of Hebron.

16 And he gave all his books and the books of his fathers to Levi, his son so that he might preserve them and replicate them for his children until this day.

[Chapter *46*]

1 It happened that after the death of Jacob the children of Israel continued to multiply in the land of Egypt, and they became a great nation, and they were in one accord of heart, so that brother loved brother and every man helped his brother. They increased abundantly and multiplied greatly, ten weeks of years, all the days of the life of Joseph.

2 There was neither Satan nor any evil in all the days of the life of Joseph after his father, Jacob (had died), because all the Egyptians respected the children of Israel all the days of the life of Joseph.

3 Joseph died, being a hundred and ten years old. He lived seventeen years in the land of Canaan, and ten years he was a servant, and three years in prison, and eighty years he was under the king, ruling all the land of Egypt.

4 He died and so did all his brothers and all of that generation. But, he commanded the children of Israel before he died that they should carry his bones with them when they went out from the land of Egypt.

5 And he made them swear regarding his bones, because he knew that the Egyptians would not bring his bones out of Egypt or bury him in the land of Canaan, because while dwelling in the land of Assyria, king Makamaron, the king of Canaan, fought against Egypt in the valley and killed the king of Egypt there, and pursued the Egyptians to the gates of "Ermon.

6 But he was not able to enter, because another king, a new king, had become king of Egypt, and he was stronger than he (Makamaron), and he returned to the land of Canaan, and the gates of Egypt were closed so that none came or went from Egypt.

7 Joseph died in the forty-sixth jubilee, in the sixth week, in the second year, and they buried him in the land of Egypt, and all his brothers died after him.

8 The king of Egypt went to war against the king of Canaan in the forty-seventh jubilee, in the second week in the second year, and the children of Israel brought out all the bones of the children of Jacob except the bones of Joseph, and they buried them in the field in the double cave in the mountain.

9 Then, most of them returned to Egypt, but a few of them remained in the mountains of Hebron, and Amram your father remained with them.

10 The king of Canaan was victorious over the king of Egypt, and he closed the gates of Egypt.

11 He devised an evil plan against the children of Israel to afflict them. He said to the people of Egypt, "Look, the people of the children of Israel have increased and multiplied more than we.

12 Let us use wisdom and deal with them before they become too many. Let us make them our slaves before we go to war and they rise up against us on the side of our enemies. Before they leave and fight against us let us do this because their hearts and faces (allegiances) are towards the land of Canaan."

13 He set over them taskmasters to enforce slavery, and they built strong cities for Pharaoh, Pithom, and Raamses and they built all the walls and all the fortifications, which had fallen in the cities of Egypt.

14 They enslaved them with harshness, and the more they were evil toward them, the more they increased and multiplied.

15 And the people of Egypt despised the children of Israel.

[Chapter 47]

1 In the seventh week, in the seventh year, in the forty-seventh jubilee, your father went out from the land of Canaan, and you (Moses) were born in the fourth week, in the sixth year of it, in the forty-eighth jubilee; this was the time of tribulation for the children of Israel.

2 Pharaoh, the king of Egypt, issued a command ordering them to throw all their newborn male children into the river.

3 And they threw them into the river for seven months until the day that you were born. It is said that your mother hid you for three months.

4 She made an ark for you, and covered it with pitch and tar, and placed it in the reeds on the bank of the river. She placed you in it seven days. Your mother came by night and nursed you. By day Miriam, your sister, guarded you from the birds.

5 In those days Tharmuth, the daughter of Pharaoh, came to bathe in the river, and she heard you crying. She told her maids to bring you out, and they brought you to her.

6 She took you out of the ark, and she had compassion on you.

7 Your sister said to her, "Shall I go and call to you one of the Hebrew women to nurse this baby for you?" And she said to her, "Go."

8 Your sister went and called your mother, Jochebed, and Pharaoh's daughter gave her wages (employed her), and she nursed you.

9 Afterwards, when you grew up, they brought you to the daughter of Pharaoh, and you became her son. Amram, your father, taught you writing. After you had completed three weeks (twenty-seven years) they brought you into the royal court.

10 You were three weeks of years at court until the time when you went out from the royal court and saw an Egyptian beating your friend who was of the children of Israel, and you killed him and hid him in the sand.

11 On the second day you came across two children of Israel quarreling together, and you asked the one who was doing wrong, "Why did you hit your brother?"

12 He was angry and indignant, and said, "Who made you a prince and a judge over us?

13 Do you want to kill me like you killed the Egyptian yesterday?" You were afraid and you fled on because of these words.

[Chapter *48*]

1 In the sixth year of the third week of the forty-ninth jubilee you fled and went to live in the land of Midian for five weeks and one year. You returned to Egypt in the second week in the second year in the fiftieth jubilee.

2 You know what He said to you on Mount Sinai, and what prince Mastema desired to do with you when you returned to Egypt.

3 Did he (Mastema) not seek to kill you with all his power and to deliver the Egyptians from your hand when he saw that you were sent to execute judgment and to take revenge on the Egyptians?

4 But I delivered you out of his hand, and you performed the signs and wonders which you were sent to perform in Egypt against Pharaoh, and against all of his household, and against his servants and his people.

5 The Lord exacted a great vengeance on them for Israel's sake, and struck them through the plagues of blood, frogs, lice, dog-flies, malignant boils, breaking out in pustules, the death of their cattle, and the plague of hailstones. He destroyed everything that grew from them by plagues of locusts, which devoured the remainder left by the hail, and by darkness, and by the death of the first-born of men and animals. The Lord took vengeance on all of their idols and burned them with fire.

6 Everything was sent through your hand, that you should declare these things before they were done. You spoke with the king of Egypt in the presence of all his servants and in the presence of his people and everything took place according to your words. Ten great and terrible judgments came on the land of Egypt so that you might execute vengeance on Egypt for Israel.

7 And the Lord did everything for Israel's sake according to His covenant, which he had ordained with Abraham. He took vengeance on them because they had brought them by force into bondage.

8 Prince Mastema stood against you, and sought to deliver you into the hands of Pharaoh. He helped the Egyptian sorcerers when they stood up and committed the evil acts they did in your presence. Indeed, we permitted them to work, but the remedies we did not allow to be worked by their hands.

9 The Lord struck them with malignant ulcers (hemorrhoids?), and they were not able to stand. They could not perform a single sign because we destroyed them.

10 Even after all of these signs and wonders, prince Mastema was not put to shame because he took courage and cried to the Egyptians to pursue you with all the power the Egyptians had, with their chariots, and with their horses, and with all the hosts of the peoples of Egypt.

11 But I stood between the Egyptians and Israel, and we delivered Israel out of his hand, and out of the hand of his people. The Lord brought them through the middle of the sea as if it were dry land.

12 The Lord our God threw all the people whom he (Mastema) brought to pursue Israel into the middle of the sea, into the depths of the bottomless pit, beneath the children of Israel, even as the people of Egypt had thrown their (Israel's) children into the river. He took vengeance on one million of them. In addition to one thousand strong and energetic men were destroyed because of the death of the suckling children of your people, which they had thrown into the river.

13 On the fourteenth day and on the fifteenth and on the sixteenth and on the seventeenth and on the eighteenth days, prince Mastema was bound and imprisoned and placed behind the children of Israel so that he might not accuse them.

14 On the nineteenth day we let them (Mastema and his demons) loose so that they might help the Egyptians pursue the children of Israel.

15 He hardened their hearts and made them stubborn, and the plan was devised by the Lord our God that He might strike the Egyptians and throw them into the sea.

16 On the fourteenth day we bound him that he might not accuse the children of Israel on the day when they asked the Egyptians for vessels and garments, vessels of silver, and vessels of gold, and vessels of bronze, in order to exact from the Egyptians a price in return for the bondage they had been forced to serve.

17 We did not lead the children of Israel from Egypt empty handed.

[Chapter *49*]

1 Remember the commandment which the Lord commanded you concerning the Passover. You should celebrate it in its season on the fourteenth day of the first month. You should kill the sacrifice before evening. They should eat it by night on the evening of the fifteenth from the time of the setting of the sun.

2 Because on this night, at the beginning of the festival and the beginning of the joy, you were eating the Passover (lamb) in Egypt, when all the powers of Mastema had been let loose to kill all the first-born in the land of Egypt, from the first-born of Pharaoh to the first-born of the captive maid-servant in the mill, and even the first-born of the cattle.

3 This is the sign that the Lord gave them, in every house on the door post on which they saw the blood of a lamb of the first year they should not enter to kill, but should pass by it, that all those should be exempt that were in the house because the sign of the blood was on its door posts.

4 And the powers of the Lord did everything as the Lord commanded them, and they passed by all the children of Israel, and the plague did not come on them to destroy them, cattle, man, or dog.

5 The plague was oppressive in Egypt, and there was no house in Egypt where there was not one dead, and weeping, and lamentation.

6 All Israel was eating the flesh of the paschal lamb, and drinking the wine, and was praising, and blessing, and giving thanks to the Lord God of their fathers, and they were ready to get out from under the yoke of Egypt and the evil bondage.

7 Remember this day all the days of your life. Observe it from year to year all the days of your life, once a year, on its day, according to all the law of it. Do not forsake it from day to day, or from month to month.

8 It is an eternal law, and engraved on the heavenly tablets regarding all the children of Israel that they should observe it on its day once a year, every year, throughout all their generations. There is no limit of days, for this is a law forever.

9 The man who is free from uncleanness, and does not come to observe Passover on the occasion of its day and does not bring an acceptable offering before the Lord to eat and to drink before the Lord on the day of its festival will be guilty. If he is clean and close at hand (near the temple) and does not come, he shall be cut off because he did not offer the offering of the Lord in its appointed season. He shall take the guilt on himself.

10 Let the children of Israel come and observe the passover on the day of its fixed time, on the fourteenth day of the first month, between the evenings, from the third part of the day to the third part of the night, for two portions of the day are given to the light, and a third part to the evening.

11 The Lord commanded you to observe it between the evenings.

12 And it is not permissible to kill the sacrifice during any period of light, but only during the period bordering on the evening, and let them eat it at the time of the evening, until the third part of the night. Whatever is left over of all its flesh from the third part of the night and onwards is to be burned with fire.

13 They shall not cook it with water (boil or seethe it), nor shall they eat it raw, but roast it on the fire. They shall eat it with care, making sure its head with the inwards and its feet are roasted with fire, and they shall not break any bone of it, for of the children of Israel no bone shall be crushed.

14 For this reason the Lord commanded the children of Israel to observe the passover on the day of its fixed time, and they shall not break a bone of it, because it is a festival day He commanded. There was no passing over from any other day or any other month, but on the exact day let the festival be observed.

15 Command the children of Israel to observe the passover throughout their days, every year, once a year on the day of its fixed time, and it shall be a memorial well pleasing in the presence of the Lord, and no plague shall come on them to kill or to strike in that year in which they celebrate the passover in its season in every respect according to His command.

16 And they shall not eat it outside the sanctuary of the Lord, but before the sanctuary of the Lord, and all the people of the congregation of Israel shall celebrate it in its appointed season.

17 Every man twenty years of age and upward, who has come on the day of the Passover shall eat it in the sanctuary of your God before the Lord. This is how it is written and ordained. They should eat it in the sanctuary of the Lord.

18 When the children of Israel come into the land of Canaan that they are to possess, set up the tabernacle (tent) of the Lord within the land occupied by one of their tribes until the sanctuary of the Lord has been built in the land. There, let them come and celebrate the passover at tabernacle of the Lord, and let them kill it before the Lord from year to year.

19 When the house of the Lord has been built in the land of their inheritance, they shall go there and kill the Passover (lamb) in the evening, at sunset, at the third part of the day.

20 They shall offer its blood on the threshold of the altar, and shall place its fat on the fire, which is on the altar, and they shall eat its flesh roasted with fire in the yard of the house, which has been sanctified in the name of the Lord.

21 They may not celebrate the passover in their cities, nor in any place except at the tabernacle of the Lord, or before His house where His name has dwelt. They shall not stray from the Lord.

22 Moses, command the children of Israel to observe the ordinances of the passover, as it was commanded to you. Declare to them every year the purpose and time of the festival of unleavened bread. They should eat unleavened bread seven days. They should observe its festival and bring an offering every day during those seven days of joy before the Lord on the altar of your God.

23 Celebrate this festival with haste as when you went out from Egypt and you entered into the wilderness of Shur, because on the shore of the sea you completed it (the exodus).

[Chapter *50*]

1 I made this law known to you the days of the Sabbaths in the desert of Sinai, between Elim and Sinai.

2 I told you of the Sabbaths of the land on Mount Sinai, and I told you of the jubilee years in the sabbaths of years, but have I not told you the year of it until you enter the land which you are to possess.

3 Keep the sabbaths of the land while they live on it, and they shall know the jubilee year.

4 I have ordained for you the year of weeks and the years and the jubilees. There are forty-nine jubilees from the days of Adam until this day, and one week and two years, and there are forty years yet to come for learning the commandments of the Lord, until they pass over into the land of Canaan, crossing the Jordan to the west.

5 The jubilees shall pass by until Israel is cleansed from all guilt of fornication, and uncleanness, and pollution, and sin, and error, and it dwells with confidence in all the land. There shall be no more Satan or any evil one, and the land shall be clean from that time forever.

6 I have written down the commandment for them regarding the Sabbaths and all the judgments of its laws for you.

7 Six days will you labor, but the seventh day is the Sabbath of the Lord your God.

8 You shall do no manner of work in it, you and your sons, and your menservants and your maidservants, and all your cattle and travelers also who lodge with you. The man that does any work on it shall die. Whoever desecrates that day, whoever has sex with his wife, whoever says he will do something on it, or he that will set out on a journey on it in regard to any buying or selling, or whoever draws water on it which he had not prepared for himself on the sixth day, and whoever takes up any burden to carry it out of his tent or out of his house shall die.

9 You shall do no work whatsoever on the Sabbath day except what you have prepared for yourselves on the sixth day, so as to eat, and drink, and rest. Keep Sabbath free from all work on that day. It is to bless the Lord your God, who has given you a day of festival and a holy day, and a day of the holy kingdom. This is a day for Israel among all their days forever.

10 Great is the honor which the Lord has given to Israel that they should eat, drink, and be satisfied on this festival day. Rest on it from all labor, which belongs to the labor of the children of men, except burning frankincense and bringing offerings and sacrifices before the Lord for days and for Sabbaths.

11 Only this work shall be done on the Sabbath days in the sanctuary of the Lord your God so that they may atone for Israel with sacrifice continually from day to day for a memorial pleasing before the Lord, so that He may always receive them from day to day according to what you have been commanded.

12 Every man who does any work on it, or takes a trip, or tills his farm, whether in his house or any other place, and whoever lights a fire, or rides a beast, or travels by ship on the sea shall die. And whoever strikes or kills anything, or slaughters a beast or a bird, or whoever catches an animal or a bird or a fish, or whoever fasts or makes war on the Sabbaths, the man who does any of these things on the Sabbath shall die. This is done so that the children of Israel will observe the Sabbaths according to the commandments regarding the Sabbaths of the land. It is written in the tablets, which He gave into my hands that I should write out for you the laws of the seasons, and the seasons according to the division of their days.

This completes the account of the division of the days.

ABOUT THE AUTHOR

Joseph Lumpkin has written for various newspapers and is author of the books *The Lost Book Of Enoch; The Gospel of Thomas – A Contemporary Translation; The Tao Te Ching – A Contemporary Translation; Encounter the Warrior's Heart; The Warrior's Heart Revealed; and Dark Night of the Soul – A Journey to the Heart of God.* Joseph earned his Doctorate of Ministry from Battlefield Baptist Institute.

Bibliography

The Book of Jubilees
R.H. Charles, London, 1902

"The Apocrypha and Pseudepigrapha of the Old Testament"
R.H. Charles Oxford, Clarendon Press, 1913

"Jubilees," The Old Testament Pseudepigrapha
O. S. Wintermute, 1983

J. VanderKam, The Book of Jubilees (2001)

Beyond the Essene Hypothesis
By Gabriele Boccancci
Wm. B. Eerdmans Publishing 1998

Look for other fine books by Joseph Lumpkin.

The Lost Book Of Enoch: A Comprehensive Transliteration
By Joseph Lumpkin
ISBN: 0974633666

The Gospel of Thomas: A Contemporary Translation
By Joseph Lumpkin
ISBN: 0976823349

Christian Counseling
By Joseph Lumpkin
ISBN: 1933589970

Dark Night of the Soul - A Journey to the Heart of God
By Joseph Lumpkin
ISBN: 0974633631

The Tao Te Ching: A Contemporary Translation
By Joseph Lumpkin
ISBN: 0976823314

The Tao of Thomas
By Joseph Lumpkin
ISBN: 0976099268

LaVergne, TN USA
03 November 2010
203308LV00001B/6/P